101 Reasons You Need to Get Rich

AF799926

101 Reasons You Need to Get Rich

by LJ Savage and ML Savage

ISBN: 978-1-7642508-0-1

First Edition

Printed by Amazon KDP

Contents

Introduction: Your Reason is Everything

There comes a moment in life—a quiet but undeniable shift—when you realise that what you've been doing to survive isn't enough to truly live. For some, it arrives during a sleepless night, staring at the ceiling, wondering if this is all life will ever be. For others, it hits like a sudden storm: the job loss, the medical bill, the dream slipping out of reach because the resources aren't there. And for a few, it's that gnawing emptiness that persists even when the bills are paid and the calendar is full—because deep down, they know they're meant for something more.

This book exists for that moment.

It's not just about money. Money is the vehicle, not the destination. The real destination is meaningful wealth—wealth that is aligned with your deepest values, that fuels your freedom, that allows you to make decisions from inspiration rather than desperation. Wealth that gives you the ability to design your life, protect the people you love, expand your possibilities, and contribute in ways that leave the world better than you found it.

Too many people treat financial goals as cold numbers on a spreadsheet: "I want to make X per year," "I need Y for retirement." But money without meaning is a hollow victory. You can hit the numbers and still feel restless, unfulfilled, even trapped—because numbers alone don't feed the soul.

The truth is this: you will only sustain the energy, focus, and courage it takes to create real wealth if you have a reason so compelling it moves you to act—even when it's hard, even when it's uncertain, even when every voice around you says it can't be done.

That reason is your "why."

Over the years, I've seen the difference between those who build lasting, life-changing wealth and those who give up halfway or settle for less than they're capable of. It's not luck. It's not always talent. It's not even the economy. The difference is that those who succeed are pulled forward by a vision that matters deeply to them—so deeply that quitting is not an option.

But here's the challenge: many people never stop to define that vision. They know they want "more," but more of what? They dream of "freedom," but freedom to do what? They say they want "security," but security for whom? Without clarity, they drift. Without clarity, they chase someone else's dream. Without clarity, they make money for the sake of making money—and wonder why it feels empty when they get it.

This book is designed to change that. Inside, you will find 101 deeply considered, thought-provoking questions—not just to answer, but to feel. These are not surface-level prompts. They're designed to pull out the layers of your desires, fears, values, and ambitions. They'll challenge you to imagine what your life could be without limitations, to confront what's truly important, and to define wealth on your terms.

And here's the key: every question is framed not as a "how"—because strategies will change over time—but as a "why." When your "why" is strong enough, you will find the "how."

Most financial advice skips straight to the "how." How to save. How to invest. How to budget. How to start a business. Those tactics are essential—but if you start there, you're building on unstable ground. Without a clear reason, you'll abandon your plan the moment it gets uncomfortable. You'll cut corners. You'll self-sabotage. You'll be tempted to chase quick wins that don't align with your bigger vision.

But when your reason is clear—so clear you can feel it in your bones—everything changes. You'll say no to distractions because you're protecting something important. You'll take calculated risks because the potential reward isn't just money—it's the life you want. You'll keep going when it's hard because you know exactly what's at stake.

101 Reasons You Need to Get Rich

Your reason is what keeps you in the game when the novelty wears off. It's what gets you back up after failure. It's what transforms discipline from drudgery into devotion. That's why this book doesn't just aim to help you make money—it's here to help you make money mean something.

The Structure of the Journey

The questions in this book are grouped into six core themes—each one representing a dimension of life that wealth can transform when it's pursued intentionally:

Section 1 — , Freedom & Security and Certainty

The ability to live on your own terms, free from financial fear, with the security to protect what matters.

Section 2 — , Variety & Adventure

The experiences, spontaneity, and exploration that keep life exciting and your spirit alive.

Section 3 — , Love & Connection

The relationships and shared moments that give life its deepest meaning.

Section 4 — , Individuality & Significance

The legacy you create, the impact you make, and the mark you leave on the world.

Section 5 — , Growth

The personal evolution that comes from expanding your skills, knowledge, and horizons.

Section 6 — , Contribution

The ability to give back, solve problems, and change lives in ways only you can.

How to Use This Book

This is not a book you rush through in one sitting. It's a book to sit with, to let the questions stir something inside you. You might find that one question stops you in your tracks, forcing you to confront something you've avoided. Another might ignite a burst of excitement, revealing a dream you'd forgotten or never dared to say out loud.

Don't just answer with your head—answer with your heart. Write down your responses. Let them be messy. Let them be raw. Then, revisit them over time. As your circumstances change, your answers may evolve—but the process of returning to your "why" will keep you anchored.

When you connect deeply with your reasons for building wealth, everything else in life shifts. Your daily choices become intentional. Your relationships become richer. Your opportunities multiply—because people are drawn to someone who knows exactly where they're going.

And here's the most important thing: your reason will not just change your life—it will change the lives of those around you. When you live with purpose, you give others permission to do the same. Your courage becomes contagious. Your success becomes a blueprint. Your impact becomes part of a legacy that outlives you.

By the time you reach the last page of this book, you will not only have a clear picture of what wealth means to you—you'll feel it. You'll see it. You'll own it. And once you do, you'll find that the steps you need to take—the "how"—will feel obvious.

But first, you must be willing to go deep. Be honest with yourself. Be willing to dream bigger than feels comfortable. Be willing to admit what you truly want—not what you think you should want.

Because the truth is, you get one life. And the cost of not finding your reason is far higher than the cost of pursuing it.

So take a deep breath. Open your mind. And let these questions guide you—not just to more money, but to more meaning.

Your future self—and everyone whose life you will touch—will thank you.

Section 1 — Freedom & Security and Certainty

The ability to live on your own terms, free from financial fear, with the security to protect what matters.

Introduction

Freedom is not just the absence of limits; it's the presence of possibility. It's the moment you realise your life is no longer dictated by a constant calculation of "Can I afford this?" or "What will happen if…?" Security is knowing that, no matter what storms rise, you stand on solid ground. And certainty? It's the rare gift of walking through life with a steady heartbeat, unshaken by the unknown.

Money, when earned and used with intention, becomes more than a means of transaction—it becomes the scaffolding that holds up the life you truly want to live. It is the quiet strength behind your choices, the safety net beneath your leaps, and the compass that lets you dream without fear of falling.

Imagine a life where your energy is no longer drained by the grind of survival, but channelled into the things that make you feel alive. Where you can say yes to opportunity, no to compromise, and trust that tomorrow will not pull the rug from beneath your feet. In this section, we explore why building wealth is not about excess—it's about crafting a foundation so stable that you can finally live without hesitation.

1.How could wealth empower you to live life entirely on your own terms?

To live life entirely on your own terms is to experience a profound freedom that few ever truly attain. It means waking up each morning knowing your choices are guided by passion and purpose—not by bills, obligations, or the fear of scarcity. Wealth, when earned ethically and managed wisely, is not the destination but the powerful vehicle that makes such autonomy possible.

Financial abundance gives you the ability to design a life that reflects your deepest values. You can choose meaningful work over work that simply pays the bills. You can live in the city that inspires you, travel to the places that spark your imagination, and spend your days with people who energize and uplift you. Your time becomes yours again—time to invest in self-development, to create, to rest, or to contribute to causes you believe in.

Wealth also builds a buffer between you and life's unpredictability. Without the constant pressure of "how will I afford this?", you can take bold leaps—launching a business, pursuing an advanced degree, or taking a sabbatical to recharge. The fear of failure loses its grip because you have the resources to recover and try again.

Living on your own terms is not about reckless indulgence; it is about intentional choice. It's about having the freedom to prioritize what matters most, whether that's family dinners every night, solo travel across continents, or philanthropy that leaves a mark on the world. It's the ability to say no without fear, and to say yes without hesitation.

This empowerment extends beyond you. When you live authentically and autonomously, you become an example to those around you—showing your children, peers, and community that life doesn't have to be dictated by external limitations. You demonstrate that with discipline, vision, and the right tools, you can break free from cycles of financial survival and live with purpose.

Wealth enables you to shift from a reactive life—constantly responding to emergencies and obligations—to a proactive one, where you chart the course. You can align your actions with your inner compass, turning dreams into plans and plans into reality.

Ultimately, to live life entirely on your own terms is to reclaim your most valuable resource: your freedom. And wealth is the foundation that gives you the confidence, stability, and opportunity to live fully, without compromise, in alignment with who you truly are.

2. What impact could you have on your family's future if you built generational wealth?

Generational wealth is more than money—it is a legacy. It's the bridge between the struggles of the present and the opportunities of the future. When you build wealth that extends beyond your lifetime, you are planting seeds for trees under whose shade you may never sit, but where your children, grandchildren, and even great-grandchildren can thrive.

Imagine your children starting life free from the heavy chains of debt. They can choose a career based on passion and purpose rather than on which job will cover student loans or keep the lights on. They can buy a home when they are ready, without years of financial stress. They can start businesses, travel, explore, and take calculated risks without the paralyzing fear of financial ruin. You are not just giving them money—you are giving them options.

Generational wealth means you can create educational endowments, trust funds, or investment portfolios that grow over decades, multiplying the impact of your initial efforts. Each generation benefits from the security and stability you set in motion, and they can then add to and expand that legacy. This creates a ripple effect: one generation's foundation becomes the next generation's launchpad.

The impact is not only financial—it's cultural. By building wealth, you have the opportunity to pass down financial literacy, discipline, and vision. Your children learn not only how to enjoy the benefits of wealth but how to manage, protect, and grow it. You teach them to see money as a tool for freedom, impact, and contribution, rather than as something to be feared, wasted, or chased without purpose.

Generational wealth also gives you the ability to protect your family from life's storms. Economic downturns, unexpected illnesses, and emergencies become manageable challenges rather than life-altering crises. With resources in place, you can ensure that no one in your family is forced to compromise their dreams due to financial hardship.

Perhaps the most profound impact is the ability to change the narrative of your family's history. If your lineage has been marked by struggle, scarcity, or limited opportunities, your actions can rewrite that story. You become the person who shifts the trajectory, who transforms "we can't" into "we can" for every generation that follows.

Building generational wealth is not about hoarding money—it's about empowerment. It's about ensuring that those who come after you have the means to live with dignity, to dream bigger, and to create their own legacies. It's about contribution, stability, and hope.

In the end, the greatest gift you can give your family is not just your love and guidance, but the freedom and resources to create a life on their own terms. Generational wealth makes that possible. It is the ultimate act of foresight, care, and responsibility—a gift that grows, protects, and empowers long after you are gone.

3.How could you ensure your loved ones never face financial hardship?

Ensuring your loved ones never face financial hardship is one of the most powerful motivators to create and preserve wealth. It's about transforming your success into a shield that protects those you care about, not just in moments of crisis, but throughout their lives.

Financial hardship is not only about the absence of money—it's about the stress, the lost opportunities, and the compromises that come when survival takes precedence over growth. By building and managing wealth intentionally, you can make sure your family has the stability to withstand life's inevitable challenges without sacrificing their dreams or dignity.

The first step is creating a strong financial safety net. This includes well-funded emergency savings, comprehensive insurance coverage, and access to resources that can be tapped instantly if needed. Imagine the relief of knowing that if a loved one loses a job, faces unexpected medical expenses, or needs to relocate for better opportunities, you can provide immediate, tangible help without destabilising your own financial security.

But safeguarding your family from hardship goes beyond reacting to emergencies—it's about proactive planning. You can

establish trusts, investment accounts, or family funds that not only cover short-term needs but also grow over time to ensure long-term stability. These resources can fund education, help start businesses, or provide down payments for homes, creating opportunities that might otherwise be out of reach.

Education is another vital component. By passing on financial literacy and money management skills, you empower your loved ones to make smart choices and avoid the pitfalls of debt, overspending, or poor investments. Wealth isn't just about giving money—it's about giving the knowledge and confidence to handle it wisely.

This commitment to protection also includes preparing for the unexpected. Estate planning, wills, and clear legal structures ensure that your assets are transferred smoothly and according to your wishes, without burdening your family with disputes or unnecessary legal costs. These steps remove uncertainty and allow your loved ones to focus on healing and rebuilding when life throws challenges their way.

The emotional impact of such protection cannot be overstated. When your family knows they are financially secure, they can take calculated risks—pursuing education, launching a passion project, or changing careers—without the fear of catastrophic failure. They can live more fully, knowing they have the freedom to chase opportunity rather than being trapped in survival mode.

Most importantly, providing this safety net changes the family dynamic. Instead of cycles of financial stress passing from one generation to the next, you create a culture of stability, resilience, and ambition. Your loved ones can build on your foundation, creating even more wealth and security for the generations to come.

Ensuring your family never faces financial hardship isn't about spoiling them or removing all struggle—it's about removing unnecessary, debilitating struggle. It's about enabling them to face life's challenges from a position of strength. That is a gift worth working for, saving for, and building for—a reason to make money that transcends personal gain and becomes a legacy of care, stability, and empowerment

4.How might you provide housing or education for those you care about?

Providing housing or education for the people you care about is one of the most transformative ways to use wealth. These two pillars—shelter and learning—form the foundation of stability, dignity, and opportunity. By offering them to loved ones, you don't just give temporary relief; you empower them to build better lives for themselves and for the generations that follow.

A secure, stable home is more than bricks and mortar. It's a sanctuary—a place where families can feel safe, rest, and grow without the stress of unstable living conditions or unaffordable rent. By using your wealth to provide housing—whether that means buying a home for your parents, helping your children secure their first property, or investing in multi-generational housing—you give those you love the foundation to live without the constant anxiety of where they'll sleep next month. This kind of stability has a ripple effect: children thrive in school when they live in a safe, consistent environment, and adults are free to focus on career growth, health, and family life.

Education, likewise, is a gift that transforms lives long after the tuition is paid. By funding a loved one's education, you're not just covering costs—you're opening doors that may have been locked due to financial limitations. You give them the ability to pursue their chosen field, to compete on a level playing field, and to earn an income that provides independence and self-respect. Education doesn't only benefit the individual—it elevates families, strengthens communities, and fuels progress.

The power of combining these two gifts—housing and education—is immense. Together, they create a safety net and a springboard. Housing provides security; education provides mobility. One keeps your loved ones grounded; the other gives them the wings to rise.

Achieving this requires planning and intentional wealth-building. You might invest in real estate with the aim of gifting or leasing properties to family members at low or no cost. You might set up education funds, scholarships, or trusts that ensure tuition is covered for future generations. Even smaller contributions—like paying down a family member's mortgage or covering a semester of school—can make an extraordinary difference in someone's trajectory.

Beyond the financial aspect, there is an emotional and symbolic weight to these acts. Providing a home says, "You have a place in the world that's yours." Funding education says, "I believe in your potential, and I want to see you succeed." These messages of support and belief can be as powerful as the resources themselves.

When you use your wealth to provide housing or education for those you care about, you're investing not only in their present comfort but in their future possibilities. You're breaking cycles of instability or limited opportunity and replacing them with a foundation of security and a pathway to growth. It's an act of love, vision, and empowerment—a reason to make money that carries meaning far beyond

5.How could you help develop a secure financial foundation for yourself and your family?

Developing a secure financial foundation for yourself and your family is not just about amassing wealth—it's about creating a structure that can weather economic storms, provide stability through generations, and open doors to opportunity. It's building a financial bedrock strong enough to stand the test of time, while flexible enough to adapt to life's inevitable changes.

It starts with clarity. You need a clear vision of what financial security means for you. For some, it's owning a home outright and having no debt; for others, it's building multiple streams of income that ensure cash flow regardless of the economy. Whatever your vision, it should be rooted in both protection and growth.

Protection comes from establishing safety nets—emergency funds, insurance coverage, and legal protections like wills and trusts. An emergency fund ensures that unexpected expenses—medical bills, job loss, urgent repairs—don't derail your financial stability. Insurance shields you from catastrophic losses, while legal structures ensure that your assets are transferred smoothly and protected from unnecessary taxation or disputes.

Growth comes from investing wisely. A secure financial foundation requires assets that appreciate over time and generate income. This might include stocks, bonds, real estate, or business ownership. The goal is diversification—spreading your investments across different asset classes to reduce risk and increase stability.

For your family, this foundation is both financial and educational. Teaching your loved ones the principles of money management, saving, and investing is as important as providing the money itself. Financial literacy ensures that the resources you build are used wisely and sustained for future generations.

It's also about creating systems that endure. Family trusts, investment accounts, and clearly defined estate plans are tools to keep wealth intact and working toward shared goals. These systems allow you to provide for your family not just today, but decades from now.

Developing a secure financial foundation isn't solely about defense—it's about empowerment. It gives you the freedom to make choices from a position of strength: to change careers without fear, to fund your children's education without debt, to retire when you choose, and to contribute to causes you believe in.

The impact extends far beyond money. A secure foundation changes the way your family lives and thinks. It replaces financial anxiety with confidence, scarcity with possibility, and instability with resilience. Your loved ones can focus on growth, creativity, and contribution because they're not weighed down by the constant pressure of survival.

Ultimately, building a secure financial foundation is an act of love and foresight. It says to your family: "You are safe. You have options. You can dream bigger." And it says to yourself: "I have built something lasting." It's a reason to make money that transcends personal comfort and becomes a legacy of stability, opportunity, and empowerment for generations to come.

6.What personal freedoms could you enjoy without financial limitations?

Imagine a life where you don't wake up calculating the cost of every choice before you even brush your teeth. Where the voice in your head that once whispered "Can I afford this?" has gone completely silent. That's not just about money—it's about liberation. Wealth, in its truest form, is the removal of invisible chains you didn't even realise you were wearing.

Without financial limitations, time stops being a transaction. You're no longer exchanging hours of your life for the bare minimum to survive—you're investing them in experiences that matter to you. Time becomes a canvas, not a deadline. You could devote your mornings to writing, afternoons to your children, evenings to learning a language you've always loved, simply because the clock no longer belongs to anyone else.

Geography opens up like a map with no boundaries. You can choose to live where the air feels right in your lungs, where the view outside your window inspires you, or where your loved ones need you most. You're no longer bound to a postcode that fits your budget but not your heart. If the seasons call you to the mountains in the winter and the ocean in the summer, you can follow them.

The ability to say "no" becomes one of your greatest luxuries. Without financial pressure, you can walk away from toxic workplaces, undervalued contracts, or draining relationships. You can set boundaries without fear, choosing only to invest your energy in people and projects that nourish you. That's not arrogance—it's self-respect given room to breathe.

Your personal growth becomes limitless. You can explore interests that hold no promise of profit but every promise of joy. Study art history, learn astrophotography, take dance lessons, or train for a marathon—not because they lead somewhere, but because they make you feel alive. Financial freedom turns curiosity into an open door instead of a dead end.

Perhaps the most underrated freedom is mental peace. Without the constant hum of money worries, your mind is free to think, create, dream, and connect. You can live in the present without the shadow of the next bill, the next payment, the next "what if." That clarity allows you to make decisions from a place of intention rather than desperation.

In the end, personal freedom isn't about having everything—it's about having choice. It's the power to shape your life in alignment with your values, to craft each day like a work of art instead of rushing through it like a to-do list. When money no longer dictates the terms, you finally get to decide what the story of your life will be. And there is no greater freedom than being the author of your own days.

7.How might you protect your lifestyle from unexpected crises?

Life has a way of testing us without warning. Illness, job loss, economic downturns, natural disasters—these moments don't wait for a convenient time to strike. When they come, they don't just challenge your bank account—they threaten the life you've worked so hard to build. That's why protecting your lifestyle isn't about paranoia—it's about honouring the life you've created and refusing to let it be swept away in a single gust of bad fortune.

The lifestyle you've built represents years of effort, sacrifice, and vision. It's the safe home you've nurtured, the routines that bring you peace, the opportunities you've carved out for yourself and your loved ones. Losing it isn't just about losing "things"—it's about losing the environment that supports your well-being, your relationships, and your future.

Wealth acts as a buffer between you and the chaos. It gives you the ability to withstand the shock without dismantling everything you've created. It means that when the unexpected happens, you don't have to uproot your children from their school, sell off cherished possessions, or abandon plans you've worked toward for years.

More than anything, it's about dignity. Crisis without resources can strip away your power to choose. It can force you into decisions that compromise your values or long-term goals. But when you have financial stability, you face storms with options—choices that keep you aligned with the life you want to live rather than one dictated by survival.

Protecting your lifestyle also protects your sense of identity. For many, our surroundings, our work, and our daily rhythms are deeply tied to who we are. Sudden loss can fracture that identity, leaving you feeling disoriented and powerless. Wealth preserves continuity—it allows you to maintain the anchors in your life while you navigate the changes you didn't ask for.

There's also a ripple effect. Your ability to stay steady during a crisis doesn't just benefit you—it supports everyone connected to you. Your children feel secure. Your partner feels less pressure. Your extended family or community may even rely on your stability as a beacon when their own world is shaking.

In essence, protecting your lifestyle isn't about being afraid of what might happen—it's about respecting what you've worked for. It's about ensuring that the life you've built is resilient enough to survive the inevitable challenges. It's about safeguarding your peace of mind, your relationships, and your freedom. And it's about recognising that while you can't control the winds, you can build a ship strong enough to keep sailing.

8. How could wealth allow you to prioritise your mental health and well-being?

In a world that often rewards exhaustion, making your mental health a priority can feel like an act of rebellion. Yet without it, every other part of life suffers. Wealth doesn't buy happiness, but it does buy the space, the access, and the security to care for your mind and spirit without compromise.

Mental health is fragile when weighed down by constant financial strain. The stress of living paycheck to paycheck, of juggling bills and debts, leaves little room for self-care or recovery. Wealth lifts that weight. It quiets the background noise of worry so you can hear what you truly need—and act on it.

When you have the resources, you can choose environments that nurture you: a home filled with light, a neighbourhood that feels safe, a workspace that inspires creativity. You can step away from toxic places and people without fearing immediate ruin. Your surroundings become part of your healing rather than part of your stress.

Wealth allows access to the right support at the right time. You can see the best specialists, explore different therapies, and continue treatment without stopping for financial reasons. You can invest in preventative care, not just crisis intervention, ensuring that your mental health is maintained rather than patched together after a breakdown.

It also gives you the freedom to rest without guilt. You can take time off when you need it—not just when your employer allows it. You can structure your days around balance, building in space for movement, stillness, and connection. You can say "no" to commitments that would drain you and "yes" to activities that restore you.

Mental health thrives in stability, and wealth creates that stability. It allows you to plan your life without the constant fear of something breaking. It makes it possible to focus on long-term growth rather than short-term survival. And perhaps most importantly, it restores your ability to choose—not from desperation, but from intention.

When your mind is well, you have more to give to your work, your loved ones, and the world. Wealth is not the goal in itself—it's the enabler of a healthier, fuller, and more present life. And in a society where mental well-being is too often sacrificed for financial survival, having the means to protect it is one of the most powerful reasons to pursue financial abundance.

9. How might you create a safety net that gives you complete peace of mind?

Peace of mind is one of the rarest luxuries in life, and for most people, it's constantly at risk. We live in a world where unexpected events—a sudden illness, a job loss, a market downturn, a family emergency—can arrive without warning, and often without mercy. A safety net is the quiet shield between you and those storms. It is not merely money in an account; it is the promise that whatever life throws at you, you can remain standing.

Without a safety net, every decision is haunted by a shadow of fear. You second-guess your career moves, you avoid risks, you settle for less than you're capable of—not because you lack ambition, but because you can't afford to fall. You stay in situations that drain you because you can't afford to leave. You delay dreams because you're too busy surviving today.

But when you have a safety net, you gain more than security—you gain freedom. Suddenly, you can leave the toxic job without a panic attack over next month's rent. You can start the business you've been imagining for years because the possibility of failure no longer means total ruin. You can say "yes" to opportunities based on potential, not just on immediate necessity.

A safety net changes the way you see the world. Without one, uncertainty feels like a predator stalking you in the dark. With one, uncertainty becomes a challenge you can meet with courage. You stop seeing life as a series of threats and start seeing it as a field of possibilities. You make decisions from a place of confidence, not desperation.

It also protects something that is far more precious than money: your dignity. In times of crisis, you won't have to make humiliating compromises or rely on the goodwill of others to survive. You'll be able to stand tall, knowing you've built your own lifeline. That dignity spills into every area of your life—your relationships, your self-esteem, your ability to take calculated risks.

There's another truth: a safety net doesn't just protect you. It protects the people you love. If your partner loses a job, if your child has a sudden medical need, if your parents require care, your preparation becomes their security too. In this way, a safety net is an act of love as much as it is an act of self-preservation.

And perhaps most importantly, a safety net buys you the most valuable currency in the world: mental clarity. When you're not consumed with "what if," you can think bigger, act braver, and live fuller. You can focus on creating, giving, and experiencing life, rather than being stuck in a constant low-level state of survival mode.

Peace of mind is not a luxury reserved for the lucky—it is a choice built through foresight and discipline. Your future self will thank you, not just for the money saved, but for the life made possible because you refused to live without a net beneath your feet.

10. How could you prepare financially for major life changes with confidence?

Life is a series of chapters, and each new chapter brings its own set of demands, challenges, and opportunities. Some changes you can see coming—marriage, the birth of a child, a career change, buying a home. Others arrive uninvited—a sudden relocation, an economic downturn, a loved one's illness. All have the power to alter your path completely.

Without preparation, major life changes can feel like standing on the edge of a cliff, blindfolded, with the ground shifting beneath you. Every choice feels urgent and uncertain. Even moments that should be filled with joy—welcoming a baby, launching a business, starting fresh in a new city—can be clouded by fear when you're not ready financially. Instead of celebrating, you find yourself asking: Can I afford this? Will this break me?

But preparation transforms those same moments into milestones you can embrace fully. When you've built the financial resources to navigate life's shifts, you step into them not with trembling hands but with steady resolve. You meet change as a partner, not as a victim.

Financial preparation gives you the power to make decisions based on what's right for you, not what's cheapest or easiest in the moment. It means you can choose the better neighbourhood for your children's education, even if it costs more. You can take time off work to care for a loved one without risking financial ruin. You can accept the dream job offer in another city without worrying about how you'll manage the moving expenses.

It's not just about money—it's about control. Preparation means you get to set the pace of your transitions. You're not rushed into signing bad contracts, taking on crippling debt, or making compromises you'll regret later. You have the luxury of thinking clearly, weighing options, and making decisions that align with your values.

Confidence during change is also deeply emotional. When you know you're financially prepared, fear no longer dictates your actions. You can focus on the experience itself—the joy of a wedding, the thrill of building a home, the pride of starting a business—instead of constantly scanning for the financial fallout. Preparation turns life changes into opportunities to grow, rather than traps that shrink your world.

And there's a ripple effect. Your calm confidence reassures your family. Your children learn, by watching you, that change is not something to fear when you plan for it. Your partner feels the relief of facing transitions with a teammate who is grounded and capable. Even your friends and colleagues see you as someone who navigates life with resilience—and that inspires them to aim higher too.

Major life changes are inevitable. Some will come by choice, others by chance. But when you prepare, you give yourself the ability to meet each one on your own terms. You claim the right to write your story, rather than having it written for you by circumstance. And perhaps that's the greatest gift financial readiness can offer: the confidence to greet change not with dread, but with open arms.

11. What steps could you take to eliminate financial anxiety permanently?

Financial anxiety is a silent thief. It steals your sleep, your focus, your joy, and even your relationships. It lurks in the back of your mind when you're trying to work, interrupts family dinners, and creeps into moments that should be peaceful. It's not always about poverty—even people with decent incomes can feel its grip if they're living without a sense of stability or control.

The importance of eliminating this anxiety is bigger than just feeling "calm about money." It's about reclaiming your mental and emotional freedom. Constant money worries can cause chronic stress, which damages your health over time. It raises blood pressure, triggers anxiety disorders, and weakens your immune system. Over years, it can erode your overall well-being—making you less present, less joyful, and less capable of living the life you want.

When you remove financial anxiety, you do more than solve a practical problem; you open up mental space for creativity, vision, and deep human connection. Imagine the mental bandwidth you'd have if you weren't constantly calculating bills in your head or worrying about the next unexpected expense. That space can be used to plan your future, strengthen relationships, and pursue the work that truly matters to you.

Freedom from financial anxiety also changes the way you show up in the world. You negotiate better because you're not desperate. You take smarter risks because you're not paralysed by "what if." You set boundaries in your career and personal life because you no longer fear the financial fallout of saying "no." That confidence ripples into every choice you make.

And let's not ignore the impact on the people around you. Children raised in financially stable households tend to perform better academically, feel safer emotionally, and dream bigger because they see possibility, not scarcity. Partners in financially secure relationships fight less and collaborate more. Even friendships improve when money stress isn't distorting your priorities or creating resentment.

Ultimately, eliminating financial anxiety is about giving yourself permission to live in the present without fear of the future. It's about waking up in the morning knowing that, no matter what happens, you have built the resilience to handle it. That knowledge allows you to enjoy life's moments more deeply and approach the future with confidence rather than dread.

When financial peace replaces financial anxiety, you don't just survive—you thrive. And thriving is where your best life begins.

12. How might you ensure your retirement years are stress-free and abundant?

Retirement is often imagined as a golden era—lazy mornings, travel, hobbies, and time with loved ones. But for too many people, it becomes a time of quiet struggle. The difference between those two realities isn't luck; it's preparation. Ensuring your retirement is stress-free and abundant is one of the most important financial goals you can set, because it safeguards not just your future, but the final decades of your life.

Why does this matter so much? Because retirement is the one stage of life you cannot easily "fix" once you're in it. In your younger years, you can bounce back from financial mistakes with time, energy, and opportunity. But in retirement, those options shrink. Your ability to earn may be reduced, your health may be more fragile, and your needs may be greater. Preparing now is an act of compassion for your future self.

A stress-free retirement means freedom—freedom to choose how you spend your days, where you live, and what adventures you pursue. Without financial constraints, you can travel, explore new hobbies, and give back to causes you care about. It also means you can support your children or grandchildren if needed without sacrificing your own comfort or security.

Financial abundance in retirement also protects your dignity. No one wants to spend their later years dependent on reluctant family members or government aid. The ability to pay for quality healthcare, a safe and comfortable home, and enriching experiences is not about extravagance—it's about maintaining independence and choice.

There's also a deeper emotional reason: peace of mind. Knowing you have enough to live well removes a huge layer of uncertainty. You can focus on enjoying the people and activities that matter most, instead of counting pennies or worrying about outliving your savings. This peace allows you to be more generous with your time, energy, and even your resources, making your later years a time of legacy-building.

And finally, an abundant retirement isn't just for you—it's a gift to your loved ones. It spares them the burden of worrying about your well-being or financially supporting you. Instead, they get to enjoy your company without the weight of financial strain, and you get to enjoy theirs with the joy of knowing you've planned well.

Retirement can be a chapter of freedom, joy, and deep fulfilment—but only if you choose to make it so. The preparation you do today is the bridge between the life you hope for and the life you will actually live.

13. How could you protect your assets for future generations?

What you build in your lifetime can echo long after you're gone. Protecting your assets for future generations isn't about greed or hoarding—it's about stewardship. It's the recognition that your efforts, sacrifices, and wisdom don't have to end with you. They can become the foundation on which your children, grandchildren, and even people you'll never meet can stand taller and dream bigger.

When you secure what you've built, you're preserving more than money—you're preserving possibilities. The house you paid off, the business you nurtured, the investments you grew—all of these can be transformed into tools of empowerment for those who follow. Instead of starting from scratch, the next generation can start from stability. They can focus on creating, innovating, and contributing, rather than fighting just to survive.

There is also an emotional legacy at stake. Passing down protected assets tells your loved ones: "You mattered enough for me to think of you beyond my own lifetime." That message carries weight. It instils a sense of responsibility, pride, and belonging. It weaves your story into theirs and gives them a tangible reminder that they come from resilience and foresight.

When families don't protect their assets, history can repeat cycles of hardship. Without preparation, one illness, one lawsuit, or one bad decision can erase decades of work. Protecting your wealth is a way of breaking generational curses and replacing them with generational momentum. It's giving the next generation a springboard instead of a safety net with holes.

Your legacy also influences the wider community. Strong, secure families are more likely to fund scholarships, start businesses, create jobs, and give to causes that matter. Protecting assets isn't selfish—it's the seed of broader impact. The more prepared and financially secure your family is, the more they can reach beyond themselves to improve the world around them.

Ultimately, asset protection is an act of love in its purest form. It's saying, "I worked for this, but it's not just for me." It's knowing that you're part of a continuum, that what you plant now will be shade for someone else years from today. Protecting your assets for future generations is about turning your life's work into a legacy of stability, opportunity, and hope.

14. How might you plan for emergencies without disrupting your lifestyle?

Emergencies don't just test your finances—they test your peace. They arrive without warning, threatening to knock you off the path you've worked so hard to carve. The reason it's important to plan for them isn't simply about having "extra money." It's about preserving the life you've built, even when the ground shakes beneath you.

Your lifestyle is more than your spending habits—it's the rhythm of your days, the comfort of your routines, the environment you've chosen for yourself and your loved ones. When an emergency strikes, the true cost isn't just the bill—it's the disruption to your stability, identity, and well-being. Planning for these moments protects not only your assets, but also your sense of self.

When you're unprepared, emergencies can force you into choices you wouldn't otherwise make—selling something you cherish, taking on work you hate, or abandoning long-term goals just to plug a short-term hole. Planning in advance means you can meet life's surprises without surrendering what matters most. It means you can handle the storm without dismantling the house.

There's also a psychological weight to consider. Knowing you can weather a crisis without tearing apart your life gives you freedom in the present. You can make bolder decisions, take calculated risks, and embrace new opportunities because you're not haunted by "What if?" That sense of security doesn't just help you in emergencies—it changes how you live every single day.

And let's not forget the people around you. When you're prepared, you're not just protecting yourself—you're shielding your family from unnecessary upheaval. Children can stay in the same school, partners can focus on solutions instead of panic, and your relationships can remain grounded in stability instead of stress.

Planning for emergencies without disrupting your lifestyle is, at its heart, about protecting the life you've chosen from being undone in moments you can't control. It's a way of saying: "This is my life, and I will not let circumstance dictate its course."

15. What investments could make your income truly resilient?

Resilience is the quiet strength that keeps you standing when the winds change. When it comes to income, resilience isn't about earning the most—it's about earning in a way that endures. The reason to pursue it isn't just financial security—it's the freedom that comes from knowing your livelihood is not at the mercy of a single event, market, or decision-maker.

Life is unpredictable. Economies rise and fall. Industries evolve. Technology disrupts. Without resilient income, a single shift can unravel years of work. But when your income can adapt—when it comes from a foundation designed to survive change—you gain the power to keep moving forward, no matter what.

Resilient income means peace of mind. It means you can sleep without replaying the "what ifs" in your head. It means you're not forced into desperation if one client leaves, one product flops, or one market slows down. Instead, you can respond with agility and purpose, not panic.

It also means you can pursue your dreams without gambling your stability. You can take a sabbatical, start a passion project, or shift careers knowing your livelihood won't collapse. Resilient income isn't a safety net—it's a launchpad.

Beyond personal freedom, resilient income creates generational stability. It allows you to pass on not just money, but a model for how to create wealth that lasts. It's the antidote to cycles of feast and famine that keep so many families from building true prosperity.

And perhaps most importantly, it changes your relationship with money itself. Instead of chasing the next paycheck, you focus on building systems and assets that work for you. This shift—from dependency to empowerment—is one of the most transformative financial changes you can make.

In the end, resilient income is about more than surviving downturns—it's about thriving through them. It's about building a life that cannot be undone by a single change in circumstance. And that is a reason worth working for.

Conclusion

Freedom, security, and certainty are not luxuries; they are the cornerstones of a life fully lived. When money is managed with purpose, it gives you more than comfort—it gives you control over your own narrative. It silences the noise of fear, replaces scarcity with choice, and transforms dreams from distant visions into daily realities.

This is not about chasing wealth for its own sake—it's about using it as a tool to build the unshakable confidence that allows you to step boldly into the future. When you have certainty, you can venture further. When you have security, you can stand taller. And when you have freedom, you can live not just a life that is possible, but a life that is yours.

From here, we move to the next dimension of a rich life—variety and adventure. Because once your foundation is secure, the real question becomes: What will you dare to explore?

Section 2 — Variety & Adventure

The experiences, spontaneity, and exploration that keep life exciting and your spirit alive.

Introduction

Once your life is grounded in freedom and security, a new hunger emerges—not for safety, but for expansion. We were never meant to live the same day over and over again until our years run out. The human spirit craves variety, fresh horizons, and the thrill of adventure. It's in those moments when your heart races, when the unknown calls your name, that you feel most alive.

Money, in this realm, becomes more than security—it becomes the fuel that propels you beyond the familiar. It's the open ticket to explore the world's hidden corners, to immerse yourself in cultures so different they reshape your very sense of self, to try experiences that push you to the edge of your comfort zone and show you what you're truly capable of.

Adventure is not always about climbing mountains or crossing oceans—it's about saying yes when the moment arrives. It's about tasting life in its richest colours, collecting stories worth telling, and having the freedom to follow curiosity wherever it leads. Financial abundance doesn't just make these moments possible; it makes them limitless. And with each new experience, your world doesn't just grow bigger—it grows deeper.

16. What adventures would you embark on if cost was irrelevant?

Imagine standing at the edge of possibility, where the only question isn't "Can I afford it?" but "Do I dare?" When cost is irrelevant, the world stops being a series of locked doors and becomes a vast expanse of open gates. You're free to say yes to the kind of adventures that ignite your soul, stretch your courage, and leave a legacy of memories that money alone can't buy.

This is not about indulgence for the sake of indulgence. It's about liberation—the freedom to follow the pull of your heart without the leash of a budget. When you remove cost from the equation, you can choose experiences for their richness, not their price tag. You can take that three-month trek across Patagonia, not because it's on a travel blog, but because you've always wanted to watch the Andes turn pink at sunrise. You can learn to sail across the Pacific, not because it's "exclusive," but because it teaches you patience, navigation, and humility in the face of nature.

The importance of this freedom goes deeper than the surface thrill. Adventures shift perspective. They dissolve the walls of routine and introduce you to versions of yourself you never knew existed. Cost-free exploration removes the compromises that usually force you to settle for less. You don't just book the cheapest tour; you design your own journey. You don't just take a quick holiday; you immerse yourself in a place until its rhythms feel like home.

It also changes the way you give and connect. Imagine surprising a loved one with a trip to trace your shared family history through distant countries. Or funding a conservation project in Africa, and actually joining the team on the ground to witness the difference you've made. Money without adventure is static; money used for adventure becomes a catalyst—for growth, for relationships, for joy.

When you can pursue what excites you without the nagging voice of financial caution, your life becomes more intentional. You stop deferring dreams to a "someday" that may never come. You see the urgency in experiences, knowing that the seasons of life—your health, your family, your energy—don't wait forever.

And there's another layer: you return from these adventures different. Richer in wisdom. Fuller in empathy. More courageous in decision-making. These qualities bleed into everything else—your work, your relationships, your ambitions. They make you someone who isn't just surviving life but living it, shaping it, and passing on stories that will outlast you.

So when cost is irrelevant, the adventure isn't just about where you go. It's about who you become in the process. That's why this matters: because a life unshackled from financial limits isn't just measured in money—it's measured in horizons crossed, fears faced, and a personal map of the world that you've filled in with your own two hands.

17. How could wealth give you more freedom to travel the world and explore new cultures?

Travel is not just movement across geography—it's movement across perspectives. Every culture you encounter offers a different mirror, reflecting back parts of yourself you never see at home. But for most people, the desire to explore is tempered by the constraints of budget, time off work, and the compromises of cut-price travel. Wealth dissolves those barriers, allowing you to approach travel not as a rushed escape, but as a deliberate, transformative act.

The real gift of financial freedom in travel is choice—the ability to travel how, when, and why you want. Without the pressure of limited time or money, you can slow down. You can stay long enough in Kyoto to witness not just the cherry blossoms in spring, but the crimson maples in autumn. You can live in a Moroccan medina for months, learning the spice markets and language from the inside out, rather than just photographing them for a weekend.

Wealth opens doors to experiences that deepen connection with place and people. You can take part in a masterclass with an Italian luthier, learning to craft a violin. You can join an indigenous guide in the Amazon who shares sacred knowledge passed down through generations. These are not things that can be rushed or crammed into a budget itinerary—they require the kind of unhurried presence that money can buy.

There's also the freedom to be intentional about your impact. You can choose to stay in family-run inns rather than faceless hotel chains, or support social enterprises that give back to local communities. You can fund and participate in environmental restoration projects in the very places you visit. Financial freedom gives you the power to ensure your travel enriches not only your life, but the lives of those you meet.

Most importantly, wealth lets travel be an ongoing part of life, not a rare luxury. You can weave exploration into the fabric of your year—a few weeks in one country, a month in another—without the logistical and financial stress of squeezing it into an annual leave allowance. You can maintain a rhythm of cultural immersion that keeps your mind open, your creativity fertile, and your empathy wide.

When you return home from travels made possible by wealth, you carry more than souvenirs. You carry new ways of thinking, alternative solutions to problems, and a greater understanding of humanity's shared threads. This expanded worldview influences everything—your relationships, your work, your values.

So the reason this matters goes far beyond seeing more of the world. Wealth gives you the freedom to experience cultures on their own terms, to absorb their beauty and complexity without rushing past. It allows travel to become a form of education, a practice in empathy, and a lifelong source of inspiration. And in the end, those are the journeys that shape you—the kind that money can unlock, but only curiosity and presence can complete.

18. How might you take bigger personal risks and pursue bold ideas?

There's a certain kind of courage that blooms when your survival isn't on the line. Most people's appetite for risk is shaped by necessity—the rent must be paid, the fridge must be stocked, and any idea that threatens that baseline security gets pushed aside, no matter how compelling it might be. Wealth changes that equation. It creates a foundation sturdy enough that you can reach further, dream bigger, and dare in ways that a hand-to-mouth existence will not allow.

Taking risks isn't about recklessness. It's about trusting yourself enough to step into the unknown without the constant fear of financial collapse. With a safety net in place, you can give yourself the permission to experiment—to launch the business idea that's been whispering at you for years, to switch careers into something less "safe" but infinitely more fulfilling, to create art that may or may not sell but is undeniably yours.

The importance of this cannot be overstated, because bold ideas often live in the margins of what feels possible. Without financial breathing room, those margins shrink until they vanish. When you have wealth, you can expand them again—and in doing so, expand your life. You can embrace the kind of calculated risks that lead to extraordinary rewards: writing the book, buying the failing vineyard you believe you can revive, moving to a new country to start fresh, or funding a prototype for an invention that's only existed in your sketches.

Wealth also allows you to endure the natural learning curve that comes with risk. Many worthwhile ventures stumble before they soar. Without resources, that stumble can be fatal; with them, it's simply part of the journey. You can pivot without panic, adapt without abandoning your vision, and learn without the lesson costing you your entire stability.

And then there's the ripple effect. When you take bold steps, you give permission for others to do the same. Your risks can inspire a friend to leave a job that's draining them, or a family member to return to school, or a colleague to pitch an idea they've been holding back. This is how innovation spreads—not through theory, but through lived example.

The reason it matters to be able to take bigger personal risks isn't just about potential financial gain. It's about living in alignment with your deepest convictions instead of being fenced in by fear. It's about unlocking the kind of creative energy and personal growth that only comes when you step outside the predictable and into the possibility-rich unknown.

Wealth doesn't guarantee that every leap will lead to a soft landing. But it does ensure that you can climb again if you fall. It gives you the rare gift of being able to treat life as an experiment—one where the aim isn't just to survive, but to discover what you're truly capable of when the safety nets are strong, and the horizon is wide open.

19. How could you explore innovative technologies or industries without fear of failure?

The future belongs to those who are willing to step into the unfamiliar before it's safe, before it's popular, before the crowd has arrived. Yet the irony is that most people watch revolutions happen from the sidelines because the personal stakes feel too high. When every dollar is tethered to survival, venturing into a new technology or untested industry feels like gambling with your life.

Wealth removes that weight from the decision. It creates the breathing space to explore without the constant calculation of "What if I lose everything?" That freedom to experiment is not a luxury—it's the engine of progress. It's why those with resources often become the early adopters, the quiet backers, or the bold founders who shape the direction of entire fields.

Innovative technologies—whether in renewable energy, biotech, artificial intelligence, space exploration, or sustainable food systems—carry within them the power to change the way the world works. But they also come with uncertainty. The first wave is where the learning happens, where missteps are inevitable, and where the payoff (if it comes) may be years away. The reason it's so important to have the wealth to engage in this space is not just for personal profit, but because your involvement can accelerate ideas that matter.

When you have the means, you can fund a start-up that's building clean water solutions without fearing that a delayed return will derail your own life. You can pilot emerging tech in your own business or community without the terror of bankruptcy if it fails. You can invest in industries still considered "fringe"—not because you're reckless, but because you understand that the fringe is often where the future starts.

More than that, financial freedom changes the way you process setbacks. Without wealth, a failed venture can feel like a catastrophe you might never recover from. With wealth, it becomes an education—sometimes an expensive one, but still an asset you carry forward. You can absorb the lessons, pivot to the next iteration, and keep moving without being crushed under the weight of immediate survival.

This isn't just about personal gain; it's about being able to act on your values without compromise. If you believe in sustainable energy, you can be part of its growth. If you believe in expanding access to health care, you can support med-tech innovation. If you believe in a more connected, creative world, you can seed the tools that make it possible.

The reason it matters to be able to explore new technologies and industries without fear of failure is because the world's most urgent problems won't be solved by the risk-averse. They'll be solved by people who can afford to be brave, to test ideas that might not work, and to keep going until they find the ones that do. Wealth gives you the chance to be one of those people—to stand at the edge of possibility and lean forward, knowing that even if you fall, you have the means to climb again.

20. What unique cultural experiences could you give yourself through your wealth?

Culture is more than art on a wall or music in the air—it's the living heartbeat of human identity. It's the smell of bread in a Moroccan souk at sunrise, the sound of an Irish fiddle in a crowded pub, the weight of history in a Japanese tea ceremony, the joy of dancing barefoot at a village wedding in West Africa. These are not just "things to see"—they are experiences that change you, deepen you, and rewire how you understand the world.

The trouble is, without financial freedom, cultural immersion is often reduced to a checklist. A rushed week off work. The cheapest flights. The budget hotel that's "close enough." A snapshot in front of the landmark, then back to the grind. You see, but you don't have time to feel. You pass through, but you don't truly belong to the moment.

Wealth changes that. It gives you the luxury of time and depth—the ability to stay long enough for a place to reveal itself to you. Instead of a whirlwind tour, you can rent a flat in Paris for a season and get to know the local baker by name. You can spend a month in Rajasthan during festival season and not worry that every extra day is burning through your rent money back home. You can learn the rhythms of a place, not just its attractions.

Unique cultural experiences are rarely found in the obvious spots. They live in the late-night conversations with locals when you're not in a rush to catch a flight. They happen when you're free to accept an unplanned invitation—to a family dinner, to join in a religious ceremony, to help with a harvest. They unfold when you can afford to follow curiosity without calculating whether it will blow your travel budget.

And these experiences don't just fill a scrapbook—they expand your empathy, your creativity, and your perspective. They remind you that your way is not the only way, and that beauty, wisdom, and joy come in forms you may never have imagined. That shift in understanding is priceless, and it inevitably shapes the way you show up in your own life and work.

Wealth also lets you engage with culture in a way that gives back. You can support artisans directly, commission local artists, fund cultural preservation projects, or bring traditions into spaces where they might otherwise be forgotten. Your money becomes a bridge between worlds—honouring the places and people who welcome you into their lives.

The reason it's so important to have the means to give yourself these cultural experiences is because they are transformative in a way possessions can never be. They change the lens through which you see everything—business, relationships, even yourself. You return not just with stories, but with a richer sense of what it means to be human. And when you carry that understanding, you bring more depth, patience, and openness into every corner of your own world.

21. How might you design a lifestyle full of variety and excitement?

A life rich in variety is a life that feels alive. It's not about being constantly busy or chasing one thrill after another—it's about crafting a rhythm that keeps you curious, inspired, and engaged. Without financial limitations, you gain the power to deliberately weave variety into your days, rather than waiting for it to arrive by chance.

The truth is, monotony can quietly erode your spirit. When every week looks the same, your creativity dulls, your sense of possibility shrinks, and even your happiest moments begin to feel muted. But when you have the freedom to mix environments, experiences, and challenges, you keep life fresh and energising.

Wealth allows you to do this intentionally. It's the ability to wake up in a coastal town one month, a bustling city the next, and a quiet mountain village after that—all without worrying that you're abandoning your obligations or risking your security. It's the space to take on projects that stretch you, then balance them with periods of rest and play.

Variety isn't just about location; it's also about what fills your hours. With financial abundance, you can explore different forms of learning—art, music, cooking, design—not because they will "pay off," but because they make you feel more alive. You can work in cycles: periods of deep focus followed by adventures that refill your creative well. You can shift between social seasons, where your calendar is full of people, and quieter seasons, where you retreat into reflection.

And excitement doesn't have to mean adrenaline—though it can. It can be the quiet thrill of mastering something new, the satisfaction of helping someone achieve their dream, or the joy of stumbling into an unexpected celebration halfway across the world. When you have the means, you can say yes to these moments without hesitation.

Importantly, wealth gives you the flexibility to pivot when the energy changes. If an opportunity lights you up, you can seize it. If a path starts to feel stale, you can step away without fear. That agility is what keeps your life dynamic—you're not locked into a routine you've outgrown.

The reason it matters to design a life full of variety and excitement is because it keeps your mind open, your relationships vibrant, and your sense of purpose evolving. It ensures that when you look back on your life, it isn't a flat line but a rich tapestry of seasons, places, and memories.

A life with variety is a life where you're constantly reminded that there is more to discover—and that reminder is one of the most powerful motivators to keep growing. With the right resources, you can make variety your default state, and excitement a natural part of the landscape of your days.

22. How could you pursue spontaneous opportunities without financial hesitation?

Some of the most transformative moments in life don't come scheduled. They arrive unannounced—an invitation from a friend to join a sailing trip in Greece, a chance to collaborate with a visionary you've always admired, a seat opening up in a workshop that could shift your career. These moments are often fleeting, and the difference between experiencing them or watching them pass often comes down to one thing: whether you can afford to say yes.

Without financial freedom, spontaneity can feel like a luxury you simply can't risk. Every decision is filtered through the lens of cost, logistics, and the potential disruption to stability. Even if your heart says "go," your bank account might say "wait," and in that pause, the door can close. Over time, these missed moments can quietly stack up into regret.

Wealth changes that equation entirely. It removes the hesitation that comes from wondering, "Can I afford this?" and replaces it with the much more empowering question, "Do I want this?" That single shift can alter the trajectory of your life. You're able to respond to opportunities as they arise, not months or years later when they're gone.

The beauty of spontaneous opportunities is that they often carry an energy you can't replicate through careful planning. They can spark connections, open new paths, and infuse your life with a sense of aliveness that comes from stepping into the unknown. Being able to act on them is not just about indulgence—it's about positioning yourself in the flow of life where possibility thrives.

Imagine hearing about a last-minute expedition to Antarctica and being able to book the ticket that day. Or getting a call that a close friend is performing in another country and hopping on a plane to surprise them. Or stumbling upon an investment or collaboration that aligns perfectly with your values and being able to seize it without having to liquidate assets in a panic.

This is why it matters: spontaneity keeps you connected to the present moment. It lets you live in real time, rather than constantly deferring joy for a "someday" that may never come. It reinforces that your life is your own to direct, not simply a schedule to follow.

When money is no longer a gatekeeper, you can let curiosity lead, trust your instincts, and embrace the richness of unplanned moments. You start to see that life isn't just made in the big, deliberate moves—it's also made in the small, unexpected chances you choose to take. And those chances often hold more magic than even the most carefully laid plans.

Wealth doesn't just make spontaneity possible—it makes it sustainable. It ensures that saying yes today won't cause instability tomorrow. And that kind of security gives you the freedom to follow the moments that could change everything.

23. How might you indulge in once-in-a-lifetime adventures with loved ones?

Some experiences are so rare, so extraordinary, that they carry a weight far beyond their price tag. They are the kind of adventures that become family legends, told and retold across generations. The kind that bind people together because they were shared at a moment when life aligned in just the right way.

Without financial flexibility, these moments can feel out of reach. You might dream of taking your parents on the trip they've talked about their entire lives, but push it off because "things aren't right financially." You might want to celebrate a milestone birthday with friends on a private safari or rent a villa where your whole family can spend a week together—but the cost feels insurmountable. And then, time passes. People move away. Loved ones age. Opportunities vanish.

Wealth changes that story. It means you can seize these once-in-a-lifetime chances when they present themselves, without hesitation, without compromise. It gives you the ability to bring people together in ways that would otherwise be impossible, to create shared experiences that are as much about connection as they are about adventure.

Think of surprising your partner with a hot-air balloon ride over Cappadocia at sunrise. Or taking your children to witness the Northern Lights in Iceland, wrapped in blankets with mugs of hot chocolate. Or flying your siblings and their families to a beach house for a reunion where laughter echoes late into the night. These aren't just "trips" or "treats"—they're investments in memories that will outlive all of you.

The power of these adventures isn't only in the destination. It's in the act of saying, "We are going to do this now, while we can, together." Wealth gives you that choice. It allows you to skip the years of "someday" talk and move straight to action, turning ideas into lived experiences.

Why is this important? Because the truth is, money loses its meaning if it's never translated into moments that enrich the lives of the people you love. You could spend decades accumulating wealth, but if you never use it to deepen relationships, you've missed one of its greatest purposes. Shared adventures create bonds that can't be replicated by gifts or possessions. They live on in the way people look at each other, in the inside jokes and the shared stories that become a family's foundation.

And here's the deeper truth: time is the one resource you cannot replenish. You can earn more money, but you can't buy back the years when your children are young, when your parents are still healthy enough to travel, or when your best friends are still in the same season of life.

Wealth ensures you can say yes to the trips, the reunions, the bucket-list experiences while those windows are open. It ensures that when the opportunity arises to do something unforgettable, you don't have to let it slip away because of finances.

When you have the means to create these moments, you're not just funding adventures. You're weaving together the stories that your loved ones will carry forever—the kind that make a life feel full, rich, and deeply connected.

24. What extreme sports or challenges could you finally try?

There's a particular kind of thrill that comes from testing your limits—from stepping into something that demands every ounce of your focus, skill, and courage. Extreme sports and challenges aren't just about adrenaline; they're about transformation. They change the way you see yourself. They prove that you can go further, climb higher, dive deeper than you thought possible.

Yet for many people, the barrier isn't just physical readiness or willpower—it's financial. Skydiving over the Swiss Alps, learning to kite-surf in Mauritius, climbing Kilimanjaro with a guide, or running an ultra-marathon in Patagonia—all require resources. The gear, the training, the travel, the safety measures—they add up quickly. Without the financial means, these pursuits often remain in the realm of "maybe one day," fading into the background as responsibilities and routine take over.

Wealth removes that barrier. It allows you to chase the kind of challenges that most people only watch from afar. It gives you access not only to the sport itself but to do it in the best, safest, most enriching way possible—with expert training, top-tier equipment, and environments that maximise the experience.

Why is this important? Because extreme challenges have a way of stripping life down to its essentials. In the middle of a white-water rapid, or halfway up a sheer cliff, there's no space for overthinking or carrying the weight of yesterday's worries. You are fully present. You discover parts of yourself that routine life never calls upon. You meet fear—and move through it. You gain a clarity and confidence that stays with you long after the challenge ends.

There's also the profound satisfaction of completing something few people ever attempt. Not for the sake of bragging rights, but for the private knowledge that you set a difficult goal and met it. That sense of achievement is a well you can draw from for the rest of your life.

And let's not forget the stories. These are the moments you'll talk about decades later—the wind cutting across your face as you paraglided above a coastal cliff, the moment you touched the summit after days of climbing, the first breath you took after surfacing from a deep-sea dive. They become part of your personal legend, the proof that you lived fully, not cautiously.

In a deeper sense, pursuing these challenges is also about honouring your physical potential while you have it. Our bodies are not permanent. Strength, agility, and endurance are gifts that fade with time if left unused. Wealth allows you to seize these opportunities now, to live out the bold physical chapters of your life while you still can.

And perhaps most meaningfully, extreme sports and challenges often connect you to people in a unique way—teammates, guides, fellow adventurers. Bonds forged through shared risk and triumph are unlike any other. They remind you that, in life, the best views are often at the end of the hardest climbs.

When money is no longer the barrier, you give yourself permission to explore the edges of your courage. You stop asking, "What if I fail?" and start asking, "What might I discover about myself if I try?"

25. How might you fund a year of exploration around the globe?

Imagine a year where your address changes with the seasons, where every few weeks a new skyline greets you at sunrise, and the horizon is never the same twice. A year of exploration is not just a long vacation—it's a complete reimagining of what your life can be. It's the deliberate choice to trade the familiar for the extraordinary, to step outside the patterns that have quietly shaped you, and to see what exists beyond them.

The value of such a year goes far deeper than ticking destinations off a list. Living in different corners of the world changes your perspective in ways no book, documentary, or weekend trip can. You don't just see the world; you begin to understand it. You discover how daily life is lived in places you've only read about—the smells of the morning market, the rhythm of a local bus ride, the unspoken etiquette in a family home.

Wealth turns this vision from a wistful dream into an actionable choice. Without the financial means, a year abroad can feel impossible—responsibilities and costs pile up, and the practicalities seem insurmountable. But when money ceases to be the roadblock, the logistics transform from "how could I ever?" to "where will I begin?" You're free to design the year around experiences that truly matter to you rather than what fits a constrained budget.

This kind of journey is also an investment in adaptability—a skill more valuable than almost anything else in our unpredictable world. When you move from one country to the next, you learn to navigate new systems, languages, and customs quickly. You become comfortable in uncertainty, confident in your ability to find your footing no matter where you are. Those lessons will serve you for the rest of your life, in business, relationships, and every challenge you face.

Spending a year exploring also creates a bank of inspiration that you can draw from forever. Every conversation with a stranger, every unexpected detour, every breathtaking view becomes part of your mental library—ideas and perspectives you can apply to your work, your art, your relationships. It's like planting seeds from every corner of the globe in the soil of your own mind, and watching them grow into new possibilities.

There's another layer here: legacy. A year of exploration becomes a story you pass down. It may inspire your children, your friends, your community to see the world with wider eyes. It shows others that a life doesn't have to be confined to the map you were born into.

And perhaps most importantly, such a year is a declaration to yourself: that you're not waiting for "someday" to live the way you want. That you're willing to invest in experiences that will shape you in ways no object or possession could. When the year is over, you'll return with more than souvenirs—you'll bring back a new understanding of the world and your place in it.

Wealth gives you the rarest gift of all: the ability to say yes to the kind of adventure that transforms not just your passport, but your soul.

26. How could you experience every continent without financial worry?

To set foot on every continent is more than a travel goal—it's a statement about your willingness to live a life that spans the full spectrum of human and natural diversity. It's to say, "I will not limit my world to the boundaries I've inherited." From the ice-sculpted stillness of Antarctica to the red sands of the Australian outback, from the dense rainforests of South America to the historic pulse of Europe, each continent offers an entirely different chapter in the story of Earth—and of yourself.

Experiencing them all without financial worry changes the nature of the journey entirely. When money is tight, travel can become a series of compromises: the cheapest flights, the fastest itineraries, the hostel beds shared with strangers out of necessity. There's nothing wrong with those experiences, but they often leave you too exhausted or distracted to absorb the full richness of where you are.

When wealth removes those constraints, you're free to travel with intentionality rather than urgency. You can linger long enough to notice the subtle details—the way light filters through a Kyoto temple at dawn, the scent of cinnamon in a Moroccan souk, the eerie quiet of the Patagonian wilderness. You're not rushing to catch the next budget flight; you're present in the life unfolding in front of you.

There's also a profound mental shift when cost is no longer a shadow over every decision. You don't hesitate to detour for an unexpected festival or stay an extra week in a city that has captured your heart. You can say yes to experiences that might have seemed "too much" before—a guided trek to see mountain gorillas, a private astronomy session under Namibia's vast desert sky, a slow expedition across the Drake Passage to Antarctica.

The significance of experiencing every continent lies in the deep empathy it fosters. Once you've shared meals, laughter, and conversations with people from every corner of the globe, it becomes impossible to see the world as "us" and "them." Boundaries fade; humanity feels closer. That kind of understanding isn't just enriching—it's transformative. It shapes how you vote, how you lead, how you raise your children, how you contribute to your community.

And because you've experienced the planet in its vastness, you begin to care for it differently. The glaciers you've walked on, the coral reefs you've swum above, the ancient forests you've wandered—they're no longer abstract news stories, they're personal connections. You understand viscerally what's at stake in protecting them.

Wealth in this context isn't about luxury for its own sake; it's about freedom from the compromises that can blunt the edges of adventure. It's about having the time, energy, and presence to let each place teach you something lasting.

By the time you've set foot on all seven continents, you won't just have a list of countries visited—you'll carry within you a map of experiences, emotions, and insights that will inform every decision you make going forward. That's why the ability to explore the whole planet without financial worry isn't just desirable—it's one of the most valuable uses of wealth there is.

27. What dream destinations could become regular retreats for you?

A dream destination visited once is a treasured memory. A dream destination visited often becomes a part of your life's rhythm—a sanctuary you return to not as a stranger, but as someone who belongs. The difference is profound. When cost is no longer a barrier, those places that once seemed like rare indulgences can become regular touchstones, grounding you in joy, perspective, and renewal.

There's something deeply human about having a place in the world that calls you back again and again. It might be a quiet fishing village where the locals know your name and the café owner starts making your coffee before you order. It might be a mountain retreat where the view from your balcony never fails to reset your priorities. It might be a sunlit city where each visit reveals another hidden alleyway, another friendship, another layer of history.

Wealth transforms these retreats from "occasional escapes" into part of your well-being infrastructure. You're not rationing vacation days or calculating currency exchanges; you're building a relationship with a place that continually restores you. The magic here isn't just in the beauty of the destination—it's in the familiarity. The streets become as known to you as your own neighbourhood, yet they always feel fresh because they're bathed in the light of a different latitude.

Making a dream destination part of your life also means you can experience it in every season. You might see Paris in spring when the chestnut trees bloom, then return in winter when the Seine reflects the glow of holiday lights. You can watch the cycle of a Balinese rice harvest, or notice how the colours of the Mediterranean shift from summer's brilliance to autumn's softness. This seasonal intimacy deepens your connection to the place and lets you witness it as a living, changing being rather than a postcard.

These retreats also become creative wells. Writers, artists, entrepreneurs—anyone who needs to think deeply—often find that returning to the same inspiring location year after year acts as a catalyst for breakthroughs. The mind relaxes into the familiar beauty, freeing creative ideas that were stuck in the grind of everyday life.

And when you share these destinations with loved ones, the value multiplies. Children grow up with a second home in their hearts, friends share the same cherished rituals, and family gatherings in these places weave a tapestry of shared memories that grows richer over time. You're not just returning to a location—you're returning to the people you've become in that place, over and over again.

Making dream destinations regular retreats also reframes the concept of wealth. It's not about buying more things; it's about buying repeated access to the experiences and environments that make you feel most alive. It's about building a life with intentional pockets of renewal, where you can step out of routine, breathe deeply, and remember what matters.

In the end, the true luxury isn't the destination itself—it's the certainty that no matter how chaotic life becomes, you can always return to the places that reset your soul. And that, more than any possession, is the kind of wealth that lasts.

28. How might you live part-time in different countries for cultural immersion?

Living part-time in different countries is more than a travel fantasy—it's a way of life that reshapes who you are at the deepest levels. It's about trading the role of tourist for that of participant, allowing you to sink into the fabric of a culture until it becomes part of your own. When money is no longer the deciding factor, you gain the freedom to divide your year between worlds, learning to live as fully in one as in the other.

The power of cultural immersion lies in its depth. A two-week holiday might give you snapshots—the famous landmarks, a handful of meals, a few conversations. But when you live somewhere for months at a time, you experience the ordinary days as well as the special ones. You start to notice the rhythm of local markets, the subtle shift in the air before the rainy season, the way neighbours greet each other at dusk. These details, invisible to short-term visitors, become the threads that weave you into the life of a place.

There's also an emotional expansion that happens when you belong to more than one home. You learn patience in cultures where time is fluid, adaptability in places where nothing runs exactly as scheduled, and humility in countries where you are the outsider navigating unfamiliar systems. This kind of growth can't be bought directly—but wealth gives you the choice to stay long enough for it to happen naturally.

Language becomes another doorway. Spending months in a country gives you the chance to learn not just vocabulary but nuance—the jokes that only work in that language, the tone that changes a statement into a kindness. These subtleties connect you to people in ways that simply aren't possible from a hotel lobby or a guided tour. And those connections often outlast the season itself, turning into lifelong friendships, collaborations, and invitations to return.

Living part-time in different countries also changes the way you see your own culture. Distance creates perspective. You start to recognise which of your habits are universal and which are simply products of where you were raised. You see new possibilities for how to live, work, eat, and relate. In a sense, you become a bridge—carrying ideas, values, and inspiration from one place to another, enriching both.

There's also a legacy element. If you have children, imagine the worldview they inherit from growing up with more than one home. They don't just "learn about" diversity—they live it. They see the humanity that unites us beyond borders and understand the beauty of difference. That awareness will shape how they lead, create, and connect for the rest of their lives.

Wealth makes this lifestyle sustainable. It removes the logistical panic of funding multiple homes, navigating visa complexities, or maintaining income streams while abroad. It gives you the freedom to choose locations based on love, not cost—to spend winter in the warmth of Southeast Asia, spring in Europe, and autumn in South America if that's what nourishes you.

In the end, living part-time in different countries isn't just about changing your address. It's about expanding your identity. It's about becoming someone who carries the colours, flavours, and wisdom of many places within them—and who returns home each time with a bigger heart, a sharper mind, and a richer sense of belonging to the world.

29. How could you turn passion projects into real-world adventures?

Turning a passion project into a real-world adventure is one of the most powerful ways wealth can transform your life—not because it buys you luxury, but because it buys you permission to follow the threads of your deepest curiosity without compromise. A passion project is, at its heart, something that calls to you for reasons you can't fully explain. It might not start with a business plan or a measurable return; it starts with a spark. And wealth allows you to follow that spark wherever it leads, even if the path is unconventional.

When money is not the limiting factor, you can take your passion out of the notebook, off the laptop, beyond the "someday" list, and into the world. You can write the novel and actually publish it, not because you're chasing bestseller status but because you want to see it live and breathe. You can design a prototype and fund its creation, testing your idea without waiting for investors to validate it first. You can organise a music festival in a town that's never had one, or create a documentary about a story that matters to you.

The importance of this isn't just personal fulfilment—though that's huge. It's that passion projects fuel a different kind of energy, one that naturally draws people to you. When you work on something you love, your enthusiasm is contagious. You become magnetic to collaborators, supporters, and audiences who feel the authenticity of what you're building. That ripple effect can open doors that would have stayed closed if you'd stuck only to safe, predictable choices.

Passion projects also stretch you. They ask you to learn new skills, solve problems creatively, and step into roles you may never have imagined for yourself. You might become a producer, an organiser, a curator, or a storyteller. These roles expand your identity, showing you that you are capable of more than the version of yourself defined solely by your day job.

When those projects spill into real-world adventures, they can take you places—literally. Your research might lead you to travel across continents to interview experts, immerse yourself in a craft, or connect with communities who live the very subject of your work. Your art exhibit might open in a different country. Your conservation project might require you to spend months in a remote ecosystem. These aren't just trips; they're deep dives into experiences that enrich you beyond measure.

Wealth matters here because it removes the compromises that can dilute a project's vision. You don't have to cut corners because of budget constraints, scale back because you can't afford the right equipment, or abandon the idea because it doesn't promise an immediate financial return. You can honour the integrity of the idea—giving it the time, resources, and scope it deserves.

And perhaps most importantly, turning a passion project into a real-world adventure is a way of claiming ownership over your life's narrative. Too many people look back and realise their best ideas were left in drawers or buried under responsibilities. Wealth gives you the chance to live them, to create something that outlasts you, and to look back knowing you didn't just dream—you built.

In the end, it's not about whether the project becomes famous or profitable. It's about what it makes of you, who it allows you to meet, and the stories you get to live because you had the courage—and the means—to say yes to what lights you up.

30. What unconventional paths could you take if money was abundant?

When money is abundant, the definition of "possible" changes. Most people's life choices are bounded not by imagination, but by economics—the jobs they think they can take, the cities they think they can live in, the dreams they think they can pursue without risking survival. Abundance removes that invisible fence. Suddenly, you're free to walk paths that don't appear on the safe, socially approved map.

Unconventional paths matter because they allow you to live a life that is unmistakably yours. They free you from defaulting to the template that society quietly hands out: school, job, mortgage, retirement—with only occasional detours for "fun" that fits neatly between obligations. Money abundance means you can design a life that fits your temperament, your values, your curiosity—even if it looks nothing like anyone else's.

You could decide to work only seasonally, spending the rest of the year on projects or travel that matter to you. You could apprentice yourself to a master craftsperson in another country, not for a paycheck but for the joy of learning. You could move to a remote island to restore an old lighthouse, open a floating bookshop, or create an artist residency in the mountains. You could live part of each year in a completely different culture, blending worlds in a way that keeps your perspective alive and evolving.

Unconventional doesn't have to mean dramatic or eccentric. It can mean finally prioritising the kind of work and lifestyle that most people dismiss as "impractical." Maybe you want to become a full-time volunteer, fund your own research into an obscure topic, or make films about overlooked communities. These paths don't need to generate income because you've already built the cushion that allows them to exist.

The importance of taking these paths isn't just in the experiences themselves, but in what they unlock within you. When you step off the expected route, you learn to rely on your own internal compass rather than external validation. You get comfortable with uncertainty, with curiosity as your main motivator instead of necessity. That skill—trusting your own sense of direction—is a form of wealth in itself.

Unconventional choices also tend to attract unconventional people. By moving through spaces that aren't crowded with everyone following the same formula, you meet collaborators, thinkers, and creators who live by a different set of rules. These connections can be transformative, sparking opportunities and friendships you could never have engineered in the standard, linear life.

And there's another reason it matters: impact. When you have the freedom to take unconventional paths, you can model a different way of living for others. You show that stability and security don't have to mean sameness, that abundance can be used to create, explore, and serve—not just to consume. You become living proof that a rich life is measured by experiences and meaning as much as by financial figures.

In the end, abundant wealth isn't just about comfort. It's about the agency to decide what "a good life" means for you—and then to walk that road, even if no one else has paved it before. The unconventional path is often the truest one, and money, used wisely, is the tool that allows you to take it without fear.

Conclusion

Variety and adventure are not indulgences—they are catalysts for growth. They ignite creativity, expand your worldview, and deepen your appreciation for the tapestry of life. Without them, we risk falling into the slow drift of monotony, where days blur into each other and life becomes a checklist rather than a journey.

When you have the resources to explore without hesitation, every year becomes a chapter of discovery. You can give yourself the gift of wonder over and over again, filling your life with stories, connections, and moments that no one can ever take away from you.

Now, having seen what's possible when wealth opens the door to new horizons, we turn to something even more personal and enduring—love and connection. Because no matter how vast the adventure, the richest experiences are those shared with the people who matter most.

Section 3 — Love & Connection

The relationships and shared moments that give life its deepest meaning.

Introduction

At the heart of every human dream lies a longing that no adventure or achievement can replace—the need to love and be loved, to feel deeply connected to others. All the freedom, variety, and experiences in the world mean little if they are not shared. We are wired for connection; it's the invisible thread that gives life its richest meaning.

Yet, in the rush of survival, many people find their relationships starved of time, presence, and energy. Financial stress can create walls where there should be bridges, replacing moments of joy with conversations filled with worry. Imagine instead a life where your resources allow you to give your undivided attention to the people you care about most. Where money is not a barrier, but a bridge—helping you create opportunities, experiences, and security for your loved ones.

Wealth in this sense is not about extravagance; it's about freedom from the limitations that keep love on the backburner. It's being able to take time off to attend a child's important milestone, to surprise your partner with an unforgettable experience, to bring distant relatives together after years apart, or to simply sit in peace with friends knowing the world outside can wait.

Money cannot buy love—but it can give you the time, space, and means to nurture it. It can help you create memories that will be retold for generations, deepen bonds through shared adventures, and show the people in your life how truly valued they are. Because in the end, it's not just about who we become—it's about who we become with.

31. How could you use wealth to ensure your children have every opportunity to succeed?

Wealth, when used with intention, becomes more than a measure of comfort—it becomes a compass that points toward a future of possibility for the next generation. For your children, it is not just about having "more"; it is about having access—to the environments, resources, and experiences that shape who they can become. It is about giving them a starting line that isn't crowded with obstacles, so their energy can be spent running toward dreams instead of away from scarcity.

The importance of this isn't found in luxury. It is in the quiet, unseen doors that wealth can unlock. It means your children can explore without fear of lack—whether that's through education that challenges and inspires them, mentors who see their potential early, or travel that teaches them the world is vast and their place in it can be chosen, not dictated. With resources, you give them the freedom to discover their passions without being shackled to the question, "But will it pay the bills?"

Financial abundance gives you the power to remove unnecessary limitations from their path. Not to shield them from life's difficulties—because resilience is learned through challenges—but to ensure the challenges they face are growth opportunities rather than survival tests. It means they can take an unpaid internship that leads to their dream career, study under teachers who ignite their creativity, or access therapies and support if they face learning or health challenges. It's the safety net that catches them if they fall, allowing them to rise again without their entire future at risk.

There is also an emotional dimension to this kind of provision. When children grow up knowing that the essentials are secure, they learn to take bolder steps. They can take risks in pursuit of innovation because their foundation is steady. They can pursue careers or projects that inspire them, not just the ones that promise the quickest paycheck. Wealth provides the environment where creativity, curiosity, and purpose can thrive side by side.

And perhaps most profoundly, using wealth for your children's success isn't about creating dependency—it's about modelling empowerment. When they see you making thoughtful, strategic decisions to invest in their growth, they learn that money is a tool for building futures, not a prize to be hoarded. They learn that generosity and responsibility can coexist. They inherit not only the material benefits of your success but also the mindset and values that can help them create their own.

Ultimately, ensuring your children have every opportunity to succeed is not about handing them a scripted life—it is about giving them the stage, the lights, and the freedom to write their own script. It is about giving them the choice to define success for themselves and the confidence to go after it without the shadow of "what if I can't afford it?" looming over their decisions.

Because when wealth removes the fear of not having enough, it makes room for something much greater—the belief that the future is theirs to shape, and the courage to step into it fully.

32. What opportunities would you be able to create for loved ones if you had financial abundance?

Financial abundance isn't just about what it brings into your own life—it's about the ripple effect it creates in the lives of those you care about most. It transforms you from being a witness to your loved ones' struggles and dreams into an active participant in shaping their outcomes. It shifts you from offering encouragement alone to offering opportunities that can alter the course of someone's life.

The importance of this lies in the reality that so much of life is determined not solely by talent, drive, or intelligence, but by the access and timing of opportunities. Many dreams never die because the dreamer lacked ability—they die because the window to pursue them closed too soon. With wealth, you have the means to keep those windows open for the people you love.

Imagine being able to fund a sibling's small business idea that the bank dismissed as "too risky," not because you're indulging them, but because you see the potential that only someone who knows them deeply could recognise. Imagine helping a friend transition careers without the crushing pressure of making ends meet while they retrain. Think of the cousin who could attend the university they've worked their whole life toward without the anchor of debt slowing their future.

This isn't about fostering dependency—it's about removing unnecessary roadblocks so the people you love can run their race without tripping over obstacles that wealth can clear. It's about enabling them to focus on growth, creativity, and contribution rather than survival. And often, it's about giving them the first break—the one that sets off a chain reaction of confidence, experience, and success.

Beyond the practical, there's the emotional impact of being able to say, "I believe in you, and here's the proof." Opportunities backed by resources aren't just functional—they are affirmations of faith. They tell your loved ones that you see their potential as worth investing in. That belief can be just as life-changing as the opportunity itself.

Wealth also gives you the power to create shared opportunities—projects, trips, or ventures that draw your loved ones closer together. A family investment in a property that becomes a generational gathering place. A collaborative creative project that blends talents across your circle. Sponsoring a shared cause that unites everyone under a mission bigger than themselves. These are the kinds of opportunities that not only lift individuals but also strengthen the bonds between them.

The reason this matters so deeply is because time changes people's circumstances, but the legacy of opportunities given lasts for generations. When you help someone you love to step into their potential, the benefits don't stop with them. They ripple into their children, their communities, and beyond. It's how one act of generosity can set in motion a chain of events that you may never fully see, but whose impact will outlive you.

To create opportunities for loved ones is to turn your financial abundance into a force for shared progress. It's to acknowledge that your success doesn't have to be an isolated victory—it can be the rising tide that lifts every boat around you. And perhaps that is one of the most fulfilling uses of wealth there is: to know that your prosperity became the soil where someone else's dreams took root and flourished.

33. How could you use your resources to mentor and inspire people close to you?

There is a unique kind of influence that only comes from proximity. When it's someone close to you—a child, a sibling, a friend—you don't just see their public face, you see the hesitations, the private doubts, the quiet moments where they question whether they have what it takes. And because you know them this way, your ability to mentor and inspire them carries a weight that no outsider could match.

Wealth amplifies this influence. Not because money itself inspires people, but because it gives you the freedom to show up for them in ways that are consistent, creative, and deeply impactful. It removes the limitations that often stop well-meaning people from investing time, energy, and attention into mentoring others.

Mentorship isn't only about telling people what to do—it's about modelling what's possible. And when you have used your resources to create a life aligned with your values, you become living proof that success can be designed intentionally. The people close to you don't just hear your advice; they see the evidence of it in the way you live. They see that a fulfilling career, a healthy work-life balance, meaningful relationships, and financial stability can coexist. That vision alone can be enough to expand their own definition of what is possible.

Resources also allow you to provide access—something far more powerful than advice alone. You can connect them with networks they wouldn't otherwise reach, fund their participation in programs that build their skills, or give them the breathing space to pursue growth without the constant pressure of financial strain. In this way, your mentorship becomes both guidance and gateway.

But perhaps the most profound way wealth fuels mentorship is by giving you the capacity to listen without distraction. To take them on that week-long retreat to talk through their goals without watching the clock. To travel with them to an inspiring conference and share the experience side by side. To host regular dinners where conversations turn into revelations. When you're not worried about squeezing these moments into an overbooked schedule, you can give them the one thing everyone craves: your full presence.

And then there is the inspiration that comes from generosity itself. When people close to you witness your willingness to use your success for the benefit of others—not as charity, but as belief—it shifts something in them. It teaches them that achievement is not the end point but a tool, and that the truest measure of wealth is in how it's shared.

Why does this matter? Because the influence you have over people you love is one of the rarest and most enduring legacies you can leave. Businesses may close, investments may fluctuate, but a life changed by your mentorship will carry that impact forward, shaping the way they live, lead, and influence others in turn.

To mentor with the backing of real resources is to plant seeds in fertile ground. It's to give not only the wisdom of your words but the structure, the opportunities, and the environment for that wisdom to take root. And when those seeds grow, they often bear fruit in ways that surprise you—becoming part of a legacy that is measured not in numbers, but in lives transformed.

34. How might wealth allow you to spend more quality time with family and friends?

Time is the one resource that plays no favourites. No matter how much we desire it, we cannot create more of it—but we can choose how we spend it. And the painful truth is that for most people, financial strain quietly robs them of the time they wish they could give to the people they love most. Work schedules creep into weekends. Side hustles devour evenings. Worries about bills and obligations overshadow the few moments they manage to carve out.

Wealth changes this equation—not by adding more hours to the day, but by reclaiming the hours that have been sold to survival. When money no longer dictates every waking decision, you gain the space to invest your attention where it matters most: in the faces and voices of the people who fill your life with meaning.

Imagine what it feels like to answer a friend's call on a Tuesday morning without glancing at the clock. To take your children out of school for a week-long road trip because you value experiences more than rigid schedules. To visit your parents without having to fit it between red-eye flights and Monday deadlines. Wealth gives you the option to move from "when I get time" to "let's make the time now."

And the richness of this time is different. When you're not mentally running through a list of unpaid bills, unfinished work, or impossible schedules, you can actually be present. Conversations run deeper. Laughter lingers longer. You have the energy to truly listen, to notice, to remember the small details that tell the people in your life: you matter to me.

It also allows for intentional traditions. Weekly family dinners that aren't rushed. Seasonal getaways where everyone disconnects from devices and reconnects with each other. Annual reunions that bring far-flung relatives into the same room. You're not simply fitting family into the margins—you're building the rhythm of your life around them.

With financial freedom, even the spontaneous becomes possible. A last-minute weekend by the lake because the weather is perfect. A surprise visit to a friend who's having a rough week. A spontaneous night out without worrying about overtime the next day. The gift of wealth isn't just the planned—it's the freedom to say yes in the moment.

But perhaps most importantly, spending quality time with loved ones without the weight of financial worry sends a powerful message: that relationships are not an afterthought to be squeezed in around "real life"—they are the very point of it. When those you love see you prioritising time with them, it validates their importance in your life in a way words alone never could.

In the end, money is a poor substitute for connection—but it can be an extraordinary tool to create more of it. It's not about luxury vacations or lavish outings (though those can be wonderful), but about buying back the moments that are too often traded away. Because when you look back over the arc of your life, it won't be the hours at the desk that you cherish—it will be the unhurried meals, the late-night talks, the shared adventures, and the quiet, ordinary days spent together without distraction.

That is what wealth, wisely used, can give you: the choice to fill your days with the people who make them worth living.

35. How could you deepen your bonds with people through shared experiences funded by your success?

Shared experiences are the glue that holds relationships together. They create the inside jokes, the stories that get retold for years, the private shorthand that says, We were there, together, and it mattered. Yet in many lives, these moments are scarce—not because of a lack of love, but because of the invisible constraints of cost, time, and opportunity.

When you have financial abundance, you're not limited to the cheapest or most convenient options. You can curate experiences that are tailored, intentional, and memorable—not as a display of wealth, but as a way of saying, Our connection is worth the investment.

Think about what happens when you take the people you care about out of their usual environment. A weekend at a cabin in the mountains where the air is crisp and conversations flow over long walks. A shared cooking class in Tuscany, where you laugh over imperfect pasta and sip wine as the sun sets. A day at the theatre followed by a meal in the kind of restaurant you'd usually walk past.

These aren't just events—they're chapters in the story of your relationship.

The richness here isn't in the price tag, but in the space created for connection. When everything else—chores, deadlines, errands—is stripped away, you see each other more clearly. You learn things you'd never discover in day-to-day life. You find out how someone reacts when lost in a foreign city, or what makes them laugh uncontrollably, or which view brings tears to their eyes.

Wealth makes it easier to create these moments intentionally and regularly. It's not just about grand gestures, though those have their place. It's also about the smaller, repeated acts that weave a stronger fabric between you. Treating a friend to a surprise concert because you remembered their favourite band. Booking a spa day for your sibling because you noticed they've been carrying more than their share of stress. Inviting your family on a trip not because it's practical, but because you can.

These experiences also have a compounding effect. The more you share them, the deeper your trust grows. You create a bank of joyful memories that can be drawn on during harder seasons—a reminder of the good you've built together. They become part of your shared identity, a living proof of the value you place on each other.

It's easy to underestimate how powerful it is to be chosen for these moments. When you use your resources to bring someone into an experience they wouldn't have had otherwise, it tells them: You are worth my time, my energy, my thought, and my investment. That message is priceless.

Ultimately, success isn't just what you accumulate—it's what you enable. Using wealth to craft shared experiences is one of the purest, most lasting returns on investment you'll ever get. Long after the details fade, the feelings remain: the warmth of belonging, the joy of being understood, the satisfaction of knowing you've built something together that can't be bought in any store—connection that is as enduring as it is rare.

36. How might you invest in family traditions or gatherings that bring everyone closer?

Traditions are the heartbeat of a family. They are the steady rhythm that keeps everyone connected across the shifting seasons of life. Birthdays, holidays, annual trips, or even small rituals like Sunday dinners become the touchstones that anchor people to each other. They say, without words, this is who we are, and this is where you belong.

Yet, for many families, traditions fade not because love is lacking, but because life gets in the way. Work schedules clash, travel costs pile up, and logistical challenges make it easier to quietly skip "just this year." Over time, the absence of these shared moments erodes something irreplaceable—a sense of continuity.

With financial abundance, you have the ability to safeguard these rituals from the wear and tear of daily life. You can transform them from "if it works out" to "it will happen, no matter what." The power of wealth here is not in extravagance, but in reliability—the knowledge that every year, without fail, this gathering will happen because you've made it possible.

Imagine being able to fly in far-flung relatives for an annual reunion, removing the burden of cost from those who couldn't otherwise make the trip. Or hosting celebrations in spaces that feel magical—be it a seaside villa, a countryside estate, or simply a home that is big enough for everyone to be under one roof without feeling crowded. You can hire caterers so no one is stuck in the kitchen instead of laughing around the table. You can arrange professional photography so moments aren't just experienced, but preserved.

Financial freedom also allows traditions to grow and adapt as your family does. Perhaps the holiday trip you started when your children were small evolves into a multi-generational gathering that includes grandchildren, partners, and friends who've become family. You can weave in experiences that reflect everyone's changing interests—skiing one year, cultural exploration the next—keeping the tradition alive without it becoming stale.

The deeper reason this matters is because traditions are not just events; they are emotional infrastructure. They give people something to look forward to, to plan around, to feel connected to even when they're physically apart. In a world that moves quickly and scatters us across cities and continents, they remind us of our shared story and the people who will always show up for us.

By using your resources to invest in these gatherings, you're not just funding trips or parties—you're funding connection, belonging, and identity. You're creating safe harbours where everyone knows they can return and be embraced as they are. You're ensuring that years from now, when people look back, they won't just remember the places—they'll remember the feeling of being together.

Wealth gives you the power to make these moments a priority rather than an afterthought. And when you do, you're giving the people you love a gift that no market downturn can erase: the certainty that there will always be a time and place where the whole tribe comes home.

37. How could you provide stability for those you care about most?

Stability is one of the greatest, yet least visible, gifts you can give to the people you love. It doesn't shout. It doesn't sparkle. It's not wrapped in ribbons or posted on social media. But it is the quiet force that allows people to breathe deeply, make better choices, and grow into the fullest versions of themselves.

When you have the means to provide stability, you are essentially saying to your loved ones, You are safe here. You can stand tall because I've built something solid beneath your feet. That safety net might never be something they think about consciously, but its presence changes everything about how they move through the world.

Think of the alternative. When someone is living on the edge—financially, emotionally, or physically—every decision becomes coloured by fear. They take jobs they don't want because they can't risk unemployment. They stay in harmful situations because the cost of leaving is too high. They postpone dreams because the rent is due. It's hard to think about the long term when you're just trying to make it to next week.

Your financial resources can break that cycle for the people you care about most. Stability could mean helping them secure a safe and comfortable home so they're not constantly uprooted. It could mean ensuring there's always a reserve for emergencies—so a medical bill, a car repair, or a job loss doesn't spiral into a crisis. It could mean funding education, so their skills become their safety net, too.

But stability is not only about meeting needs in times of trouble—it's about creating the conditions for people to thrive. When someone knows they have a reliable foundation, they can take healthier risks: start a business, change careers, relocate for a better opportunity, or take time to heal from burnout. They can make decisions from a place of vision, not desperation.

This is why providing stability is a deeply loving act—it communicates trust and commitment without the need for constant words. It's the invisible scaffolding that holds someone up while they're building their life. And unlike fleeting gifts or grand gestures, stability endures. It compounds over years, shaping their confidence, resilience, and even their relationships with others.

For you, the one offering that stability, it's also an act of legacy. It's knowing that the structures you've built—whether through savings, property, investments, or even shared knowledge—will continue to shelter and empower the people you care about, even in your absence. It's a way of being present in their lives long after you've stepped out of the room.

Money can buy comfort, and it can buy convenience—but when used with intention, it can buy peace. And peace is what allows love to flourish without being constantly tested by the instability of the outside world. Providing stability is not about making others dependent; it's about giving them a platform from which they can stand taller, dream bigger, and live more fully.

That is the quiet, profound power of using your wealth to ensure that the people you care about most never have to wonder if the ground beneath them will hold.

38. What celebrations could you host that unite friends and family?

Celebrations are more than parties—they are the punctuation marks in the story of our lives. They are the moments where time slows, where laughter echoes a little longer, and where the people we love are gathered not because they have to be, but because they want to be. Wealth allows you to create these moments with a scale, beauty, and thoughtfulness that can transform them from casual get-togethers into treasured milestones.

When you have the means to host truly meaningful celebrations, you're not just creating an event—you're creating a space where bonds deepen. A birthday becomes a memory stitched into the fabric of someone's identity. An anniversary becomes a reminder that love can be celebrated not only by two people, but by the entire community that surrounds them. A graduation party becomes a declaration that effort and achievement matter, and that they are worth pausing the world to honour.

The power of a celebration lies in the way it makes people feel seen. Financial resources allow you to pay attention to details that tell each person: I thought about you. You matter here. That might mean flying in a relative who couldn't otherwise afford the trip, hiring a photographer so everyone can stay present in the moment, or creating an atmosphere so warm and inviting that no one wants the night to end.

When cost is no obstacle, your celebrations can be shaped not by what is affordable, but by what is meaningful. Imagine hosting a reunion in the place where your grandparents first met, or gathering generations on a family-owned property where stories from the past are told by the people who lived them. Imagine surprising your best friend with a dinner party where every guest shares one memory of them, or creating an annual festival that becomes part of your family's shared culture.

These celebrations can also act as bridges, uniting people who might not otherwise connect. Friends from different chapters of your life meet and find common ground. Family members who have drifted apart find themselves laughing together over an old story. In a world that often scatters us across cities, countries, and time zones, these events pull the threads of connection back together.

And the ripple effect of such gatherings extends far beyond the day itself. People leave with their hearts a little fuller, their relationships a little stronger, and their sense of belonging reaffirmed. They carry those feelings into their own lives, and sometimes they carry your example, too—learning from the way you used your success to bring people together, they might do the same for others.

Hosting celebrations with intention is not about excess or spectacle—it's about generosity of spirit. It's about recognising that the most valuable part of wealth is not what you can own, but what you can create. And what you can create are moments that become stories, stories that become traditions, and traditions that bind people together in love and memory.

In the end, the music fades, the plates are cleared, and the decorations come down—but the feeling remains. That's the real gift: knowing that, because of you, people left a little happier, a little closer, and a little more certain that they belong.

39. How might you surprise loved ones with life-changing gifts?

There are gifts—and then there are gifts. The kind that shift someone's life in a way they will never forget. The kind that doesn't just spark gratitude in the moment, but reshapes their possibilities long after the wrapping paper is gone. Wealth allows you to give in ways that go beyond generosity; it allows you to give in ways that rewrite someone's story.

Think of the power in handing a sibling the keys to their first home, knowing they'll never have to face the uncertainty of rising rents. Or in paying for a niece's university tuition, not as a loan, but as a statement: I believe in you enough to remove this burden so you can focus entirely on becoming who you are meant to be. These are gifts that do more than please—they liberate.

The beauty of a life-changing gift is that it speaks to someone's deepest need or dream. For one person, it might be clearing medical debt so they can finally sleep without the weight of bills pressing on their chest. For another, it might be funding the small business they've talked about for years but could never quite afford to start. Sometimes, it's giving time—paying their salary for a year so they can take a career break to travel, write, or recover from burnout.

Surprising someone with this kind of gift is about more than money—it's about attention. It means you've been listening closely enough to understand what would change their life in a meaningful way. You've noticed where the door is closed for them, and you've quietly prepared the key.

And the impact doesn't stop with them. A gift that lifts a single person can ripple through entire communities. Help one aspiring teacher get their degree, and you touch every student they will ever mentor. Fund one person's vision for a local business, and you might change the job market in their town. These ripples, set in motion by your choice to use wealth for transformation, can carry far beyond what you will ever see.

The surprise element matters too—not for theatrics, but for the emotional truth of the moment. When someone expects a slow climb and you give them a sudden lift, it's like handing them wings they didn't realise they already had the strength to use. In that instant, they feel not just supported, but seen. They realise someone believed in their potential enough to act boldly on it. That kind of validation can spark a confidence no amount of advice ever could.

It's easy to underestimate how life-changing your success can be for others when you have the means to give freely. But every time you do, you plant a seed of possibility—not just in their life, but in their understanding of what generosity looks like. One day, they may do the same for someone else, and the chain continues.

In the end, the greatest return on wealth is not measured in what you keep, but in what you release into the world. A life-changing gift is a declaration that abundance is meant to flow, that love is meant to be practical, and that the truest form of success is when everyone around you rises too.

40. How could you ensure the people you love feel valued and supported?

We all carry a quiet need—to know that we matter to the people who matter most to us. Wealth gives you more than the ability to provide; it gives you the capacity to express love in ways that leave no doubt about its presence. Ensuring that the people you love feel valued and supported is not about grand gestures alone—it's about weaving security, encouragement, and recognition into the fabric of their lives.

Financial abundance allows you to create an environment where your loved ones don't just survive, but truly thrive. It's the ability to say to your partner, "I've got us covered, so you can chase that dream without fear." It's the chance to tell a friend, "I believe in your vision enough to invest in it," and mean it. It's letting your children grow up in a world where they feel safe enough to take risks, because they know a safety net exists—not as a cage, but as a springboard.

When you have resources, you can be the steady presence that others can lean on without guilt or hesitation. You can remove barriers that make people doubt themselves—whether that's helping a family member move out of a toxic living situation, funding a course that will unlock their next chapter, or simply making sure they never have to choose between paying bills and pursuing what lights them up inside.

Feeling valued often comes from being seen in one's uniqueness. Wealth allows you to tailor your support to each person's individual dreams, rather than offering one-size-fits-all solutions. For one person, it might be gifting time off work to care for their mental health. For another, it could be financing the equipment they need to turn a hobby into a livelihood. For another still, it's covering travel so they can reconnect with distant family or explore a passion.

Support also goes beyond problem-solving. Sometimes it's about creating experiences that say, "You're worth celebrating." Hosting a milestone dinner, planning a surprise holiday, or commissioning something deeply personal—like a piece of art that tells their story—are ways of embedding that sense of value in their memory.

Most importantly, wealth gives you the ability to back your words with action. Love expressed in words is beautiful; love expressed in both words and tangible support is unforgettable. It tells the people around you that they are more than passengers in your life—they are co-authors, and you are willing to invest in their chapters as much as your own.

When people feel valued and supported, they move differently in the world. They take bolder steps, dream bigger dreams, and carry themselves with a confidence that comes from knowing they're not walking alone. The security you provide becomes the fertile ground where their ambitions grow—and the love you demonstrate becomes a model they'll pass on.

In the end, ensuring the people you love feel valued isn't about the money itself—it's about using money as a tool to build trust, deepen connection, and create a legacy of mutual uplift. It's the quiet power of saying, through your choices and actions, "I see you. I believe in you. I'm here for you—always."

41. What shared causes could strengthen your relationships?

There's a unique kind of bond that forms when people stand side by side, united in purpose. Wealth has the power to turn that bond into something unshakable—because when you use your resources to champion a shared cause, you're not just giving money, you're giving meaning. And meaning is the glue that holds relationships together through both the brightest and darkest seasons.

When we join forces for something larger than ourselves—whether it's protecting a forest, funding a local arts program, building a community centre, or sponsoring medical care for those in need—we transcend the boundaries of everyday conversation. Suddenly, our connection isn't only built on shared history or personal affection; it's built on shared impact. The victories of that cause become our victories. The struggles become our struggles. Every milestone reached is a memory we've made together, one that goes deeper than any material gift.

In a world that often measures worth by possessions, shared causes shift the focus to contribution. They invite you and your loved ones to see each other not just as companions in life, but as co-creators of change. Imagine partnering with your siblings to establish a scholarship in your parents' name, or pooling resources with close friends to fund a safe haven for vulnerable groups. These acts not only transform the world around you—they redefine how you see each other.

There's also a healing element in shared causes. They can bridge divides, soften old wounds, and open doors to conversations that might otherwise remain shut. People who disagree in other areas of life can find common ground in their shared desire to see children educated, animals protected, or communities rebuilt after disaster. That common ground becomes a safe space where respect and trust can grow.

Financial abundance gives you the freedom to choose causes that align perfectly with your values and those of the people you care about. You can take action swiftly when the need arises—funding relief within hours of a crisis—or sustain a cause over years, knowing that your consistent support makes a difference. You're not limited to applause from the sidelines; you can step onto the field and play an active role.

And the ripple effect is profound. Working together on a cause plants seeds of legacy in every participant. The children who see you and your friends rallying to protect a wetland or provide meals to families in need learn that connection isn't only about what we get from each other—it's also about what we give together. They inherit not just the fruits of your wealth, but the mindset that love and responsibility go hand in hand.

Shared causes are, in many ways, the purest form of collective memory-making. Long after the gala ends or the fundraising target is met, what remains is the sense that you stood together for something that mattered. That's the kind of story people tell for decades—the kind that makes relationships not just last, but deepen.

Wealth simply expands your capacity to say "yes" to those opportunities. It lets you turn good intentions into real-world action and transforms your connections into communities bound by purpose. And when relationships are strengthened by shared purpose, they're not just close—they're unbreakable.

42. How might you help family members achieve their personal dreams?

There's a quiet magic in seeing someone you love step fully into the life they've imagined for themselves. Helping family members achieve their personal dreams is not about buying their happiness—it's about removing the invisible weights that keep their dreams from taking flight. And wealth, used with intention, can be the wind beneath those wings.

Dreams often live in the spaces between necessity and possibility. Many of the people you care about might already know exactly what they'd love to do—open a small café, go back to school, launch a creative project, travel to research a passion—but the financial risk feels too heavy. When you have the resources to help, you give them permission to imagine without limits.

This kind of support is far more than a transaction. It says: I believe in you enough to invest in you. It's a vote of confidence that can transform not only their circumstances, but also their sense of worth and capability. Sometimes the belief you offer is even more valuable than the money itself, because it tells them they're seen, understood, and worthy of the life they've been quietly longing for.

Helping someone you love realise a dream creates a ripple effect. When one person in a family achieves something extraordinary, it elevates the atmosphere for everyone. It shows the younger ones what's possible. It inspires others to take their own aspirations seriously. It shifts the family narrative from one of limitation to one of possibility. In a sense, you're not just funding a single dream—you're rewriting the story your family tells itself about what can be done.

There's also an intimacy in being part of someone's dream journey. You get to see the messy middle—the challenges, the breakthroughs, the moments when they almost give up and the moments they discover they're capable of more than they imagined. Those shared experiences strengthen the bond between you, because you weren't just a spectator; you were a partner in their triumph.

And helping dreams take shape doesn't always mean grand gestures. It might mean paying for night classes so a sibling can shift careers, helping parents finally visit the place they've always talked about, or giving a cousin the startup capital to test their invention. Sometimes, it's simply covering the bills for a few months so they can focus entirely on their passion without the constant drag of survival worries.

Wealth allows you to be this kind of catalyst without jeopardising your own security. It gives you the power to say "yes" without hesitation, to act in the moment when opportunity knocks for them, and to create the kind of family culture where dreams aren't luxuries—they're priorities.

In the end, helping family members achieve their dreams isn't just about fulfilling their goals—it's about expanding the shared horizon for everyone you love. You get to stand together, looking out at a wider, brighter world, knowing you had a hand in making it real. And that's a legacy no amount of money could ever measure.

43. How could you create lasting memories with friends through travel or events?

When you look back at your life years from now, you might find that the most treasured possessions you've ever had aren't objects at all—they're the moments that live vividly in your memory. Shared laughter in a faraway café, late-night conversations under unfamiliar stars, the feeling of standing shoulder-to-shoulder with people you love while witnessing something extraordinary. Wealth, used with heart, allows you to turn these fleeting opportunities into intentional, unforgettable memories.

The power of shared travel or events lies in their ability to pull you and your friends out of routine. We all get stuck in the well-worn grooves of daily life—commutes, deadlines, obligations. But when you remove the financial barriers, you can invite people you care about into experiences that break the script. You can gather them in new places where the air smells different, the food tastes unfamiliar, and the conversations stretch deeper simply because the setting invites it.

It's not just about luxury; it's about presence. Wealth gives you the freedom to design experiences that strip away distractions so you can truly connect. It could be as lavish as a group sailing trip through turquoise waters, or as grounded as renting a cabin in the mountains for a week of board games and storytelling. The point is to create space for shared moments that are fully lived, not rushed or compromised.

These kinds of experiences become the fabric of your friendships. Inside jokes born in one city reappear in another. A song that played on a road trip years ago still sparks smiles when it comes on the radio. A meal you shared abroad becomes the one you recreate together every year. Money, in this context, is simply the tool that opens the door to these kinds of rituals—the kind that tether people together across time and distance.

There's also a generosity in making these memories accessible to friends who might not otherwise be able to afford them. Covering someone's flight or accommodation without fanfare can quietly shift their sense of belonging. It says, Your presence matters more than your ability to pay. That kind of inclusion strengthens bonds in a way that no gift-wrapped object could.

And then there's the legacy of it all. Years pass, but those shared adventures remain as markers in your collective story. You'll find that, as people grow older, they don't talk much about the things they bought—they talk about the places they've been, the people they were with, and the moments that shaped them. By using your wealth to create those touchpoints, you give your friendships something timeless: a bank of shared joy that can be revisited again and again, even when life gets harder or distances grow wider.

In the end, creating lasting memories with friends through travel or events is about more than seeing the world—it's about seeing each other, fully, in moments that will outlive the trip itself. It's about building a map of your life together, dotted not with possessions, but with experiences that will always mean more than money ever could.

44. How might you use wealth to reconnect with long-lost loved ones?

There are people whose absence quietly echoes in the corners of your life. Friends who once felt like family, relatives whose laughter you haven't heard in decades, bonds that faded not because of conflict but because life pulled you in different directions. Reconnecting with long-lost loved ones can be one of the most healing and meaningful things you ever do—and wealth can make it possible in ways that transcend convenience.

Time and distance are two of the greatest barriers to reconnection. The people you miss may be scattered across cities, countries, or even continents. They might live in remote areas, work odd hours, or face their own financial constraints. With resources at your disposal, you can remove those obstacles entirely. You can book the flight, arrange the hotel, or even host a gathering in a place accessible to both of you. The focus shifts from "Can we make it happen?" to "When can we make it happen?"

But wealth does more than fund travel—it creates the space to approach reconnection with thoughtfulness. You can take the time to write a heartfelt letter, send a care package filled with meaningful items, or plan a meeting in a setting that feels special rather than rushed. It's the difference between a hurried coffee in a busy café and a slow weekend together somewhere peaceful, where conversations can stretch and silences feel comfortable.

Sometimes, money allows you to bridge not just physical distance, but emotional hesitations. For people who have been out of touch for years, making the first move can feel daunting. A generous gesture—a surprise invitation, a prepaid ticket, an offer to host—signals sincerity. It says, I value this connection enough to invest in it. That act alone can dissolve years of uncertainty and hesitation.

Reconnecting with loved ones can also mean reuniting entire networks of people who once shared life together. You might bring together childhood friends who drifted apart, cousins separated by generations, or former colleagues who once felt like a second family. With resources, you can make these reunions logistically simple for everyone involved, eliminating the "if only" excuses that so often stand in the way.

The true gift of using wealth for reconnection isn't just in the act of meeting again—it's in what follows. Old inside jokes resurface. Shared histories gain new chapters. You rediscover parts of yourself that only exist in the presence of certain people. The years in between don't vanish, but they soften, replaced by the warmth of shared meals, familiar voices, and the comforting reminder that love—even interrupted—can be renewed.

In a world that constantly urges us forward, reconnection is an act of resistance. It says that some ties are worth circling back for, that some relationships deserve to be rescued from the drift of time. Money gives you the means to make that journey—not just across miles, but across the spaces where life once pulled you apart. And in doing so, you give yourself and the people you love a gift that can't be measured in dollars: the restoration of a bond that makes life feel whole again.

45. How could you sponsor opportunities that bring people together?

There's a quiet kind of power in being the reason people meet, collaborate, and grow together. Sponsoring opportunities that bring people together isn't just about writing a cheque—it's about creating moments that ripple outward, changing the trajectories of lives long after the event ends. When you have financial abundance, you can become a catalyst for connection on a scale most people only dream about.

We live in an age where isolation is common, even in crowded cities. People crave community but often lack the means or the spaces to find it. With resources, you can remove those barriers. You can underwrite retreats where people from different walks of life share their skills and stories. You can fund workshops, conferences, or creative residencies that draw brilliant minds into the same room, sparking ideas that could never be born in isolation. You can host cultural festivals that celebrate diversity while reminding people how much they share.

These moments matter because connection is fuel for human growth. A single conversation at a gathering you sponsor could lead to a partnership, a life-changing job offer, or a friendship that lasts decades. You may never fully see the web of outcomes you set in motion, but you'll know you were the one who made the meeting possible.

Sponsorship also allows you to champion the causes and values you care about most. If you believe in the power of the arts, you can fund community theatre productions or music camps that unite generations in creation. If you value innovation, you can support hackathons, startup incubators, or research symposiums that connect problem-solvers with the resources they need. If your passion is cultural preservation, you can sponsor events that revive traditions, languages, and crafts—keeping them alive by passing them on to new hands.

The beauty of using your wealth this way is that it's not about the spotlight landing on you; it's about the light you help others step into. Sponsoring opportunities is a form of leadership that doesn't demand control. You set the stage, open the doors, and let people bring their own magic. And in that generosity, you become a quiet architect of human possibility.

When you bring people together, you also create bridges between groups that might never otherwise meet. That mix of perspectives can break down stereotypes, inspire empathy, and plant seeds of collaboration that extend far beyond the event. In a fragmented world, that kind of bridge-building is invaluable.

Ultimately, the reason this matters isn't just the joy you create in the moment—it's the legacy you leave in the connections that endure. Years from now, someone might look back and say, We met because you made it possible. And in that moment, you'll realise that while money funded the opportunity, it was love for human connection that gave it meaning.

Wealth, in this sense, becomes more than personal comfort—it becomes a tool for weaving a stronger, kinder, more interconnected world. And there are few uses of money more important than that.

Conclusion

Love and connection are the true measures of a life well lived. They anchor us in meaning when the world feels uncertain, and they give purpose to the wealth we strive to build. When you have the resources to show up fully for the people who matter, you realise that money is not the end—it's the tool that lets you invest in the moments, traditions, and gestures that make your relationships timeless.

With your connections nourished, your heart full, and your relationships strong, another longing begins to rise. It's the desire to stand in the world as your fullest self, to leave your mark, and to know you mattered. This is where we step into the next chapter—Individuality & Significance—and explore how financial abundance can give you the freedom to express, lead, and shape the legacy you wish to leave behind.

Section 4 — Individuality & Significance

The legacy you create, the impact you make, and the mark you leave on the world.

Introduction

Beneath the universal need for love and belonging lies another powerful human drive—the desire to matter. To be seen. To have your voice heard and your unique contribution recognised. We all want to feel that our lives are more than a repetition of the ordinary—that we are shaping something that reflects who we truly are.

Yet, too often, financial limitations force us to shrink our vision. They nudge us into following paths others set for us instead of daring to create our own. They can silence our voice when we know it has something important to say. Imagine what becomes possible when the constraint of "Can I afford it?" is replaced with the liberating question, "What impact do I want to make?"

Wealth in the hands of someone with a vision is a powerful amplifier. It allows you to build projects that carry your name and your values into the world. It gives you the freedom to align your work with your ethics, proving that success can be achieved without compromise. It opens doors to stages, networks, and platforms where your ideas can shape industries and inspire movements.

This is not about ego—it's about alignment. When your inner voice and your outward actions match, when you can put your signature on work that represents your truest self, you don't just succeed—you stand for something. And when you stand for something, you naturally attract others who share your vision, multiplying your impact.

The truth is, individuality is not a luxury—it's a responsibility. Your gifts, ideas, and perspective are uniquely yours, and the world misses out when they remain hidden. Financial abundance gives you the resources to bring them to light, to turn personal vision into public contribution, and to leave a mark that lasts long after you are gone.

46. How could you use wealth to amplify your voice and influence?

Influence isn't just about having a platform—it's about what you do with it. Imagine being able to amplify your beliefs, your story, and your vision until they reach not dozens or hundreds, but thousands or even millions of people. That's what wealth can unlock: a megaphone for your values.

In a world crowded with noise, the ability to stand out requires both clarity and reach. Clarity comes from knowing what matters to you most. Reach comes from the resources to spread that message widely and strategically. With financial freedom, you can publish the book that's been in your head for years without worrying about whether it will be "commercial enough." You can produce a documentary that tells an overlooked story, sponsor public speaking tours, or create digital platforms that elevate voices beyond your own.

But amplifying your voice is not about ego—it's about impact. Every movement, from civil rights to environmental protection, began with someone willing to speak and persist until others joined in. With wealth, you don't have to wait for permission or scrape together resources. You can seed the conversation, fund the research, and give your ideas the push they need to become action.

The influence wealth affords you can extend to shaping industries, guiding public debates, and redefining cultural narratives. It allows you to be present not just in rooms of decision-making, but to be the one building the room. And when your voice is amplified with both reach and credibility, it invites others who share your values to step forward, creating a chorus where there was once only a whisper.

Ultimately, the reason this matters is simple: if you believe in something enough to fight for it, wealth can be the fuel that turns belief into a force that changes lives. And there is no greater use for influence than to make the world better in a way that reflects the truest version of yourself.

47. What kind of personal legacy could you leave if you had the resources to shape it?

Legacy is the shadow your life casts into the future—a story that continues long after your voice has quieted. Most people drift into whatever legacy the world assigns them, shaped by circumstance rather than choice. But with wealth, you get to author that story, to decide what echoes and what fades.

When you have the resources, your legacy isn't confined to a name etched on a headstone. It can live in the scholarships that help generations of young people pursue their dreams. It can hum in the walls of a community centre you built. It can breathe in the wild spaces you preserved, the art you commissioned, or the policies you influenced that changed lives on a scale you'll never fully see.

Money doesn't create meaning—but it amplifies it. If you value education, wealth allows you to create endowments that last decades. If your passion is environmental protection, you can purchase and protect land, ensuring its survival beyond your lifetime. If you believe in human rights, you can fund legal defences, advocacy campaigns, and institutions that keep fighting long after you're gone.

The most profound part? Legacy is deeply personal. It doesn't have to be grand to be powerful. It might be the quiet dignity of ensuring your family never faces the hardships you endured. It could be passing on a business that reflects your ethics and vision. It could even be writing and publishing your memoir so future generations understand the battles you fought and the values you lived by.

Shaping your legacy while you're alive allows you to see its first ripple. You get to witness the gratitude in the eyes of someone whose life you've touched. You can make adjustments, refine the vision, and ensure the torch you pass is lit with the flame you intended—not a dim flicker of compromise.

The reason it matters is because life moves fast, and when it ends, the default legacy is often whatever scraps remain of your intentions after the world has had its way. Wealth gives you the power to decide instead of leaving it to chance. It allows you to invest in the long arc of your impact, ensuring the best of you doesn't die with you.

When you think about it, legacy is less about what you leave behind and more about what you send forward. It's the seeds you plant whose shade you'll never sit under. And when those seeds grow into shelter, opportunity, or beauty for others, that's when you've truly succeeded—not just in making money, but in making it mean something.

48. How might you disrupt industries and stand out as a leader?

There's a certain electricity in being the person who doesn't just play by the rules but rewrites them. Disruption isn't about causing chaos—it's about daring to imagine that an entire system could work better, be fairer, more humane, more beautiful, more efficient. It's about refusing to accept "that's just the way it is" when you know it can be more.

With wealth, your voice carries farther and your reach stretches wider. You're no longer confined to making change in the margins. You can fund research that challenges outdated models. You can assemble teams of innovators who share your vision. You can launch companies or movements that don't just compete within the status quo, but redefine it entirely.

Money, in this context, is more than a resource—it's a lever. And when you have that lever, you can shift industries that have been stagnant for decades. You can take on entrenched interests that would silence a smaller voice. You can open doors to ideas that might have died in someone's notebook because there was no funding to prove them possible.

Why is this important? Because disruption is how progress happens. Every major leap humanity has taken—from the printing press to renewable energy—was born from someone refusing to accept limitations. And while ideas are free, scaling them is not. Without resources, even the most revolutionary concept can be buried under the weight of "someday."

Standing out as a leader in this space isn't about ego—it's about responsibility. When you have the means, you can lead by example, showing that it's possible to succeed without exploiting people, depleting the planet, or sacrificing integrity. You can set new benchmarks for ethical practice, innovation, and inclusivity, forcing others in the industry to either evolve or become obsolete.

And here's the truth: disruption backed by wealth has a ripple effect far beyond the original idea. Competitors start to adapt. Customers demand more. Regulators rethink old policies. The bar for "normal" is raised, and suddenly what was once radical becomes the new standard. That's the power of having both vision and the resources to execute it—you accelerate change on a scale that touches millions.

In the end, disrupting industries is about refusing to leave the world as you found it. It's about using your success not to blend in, but to stand out in a way that forces progress forward. When you marry courage to capital, you can be the spark that lights the fire of transformation—and you don't just stand out as a leader; you stand out as the one who changed the game entirely.

49. How could you fund personal projects that reflect your vision and values?

There's a deep satisfaction that comes from seeing an idea move from the fragile stage of imagination into something tangible—something you can touch, share, and stand behind with pride. Yet, for most people, personal projects get trapped in the limbo of "someday." They're postponed by bills, by obligations, by the feeling that dreams should be squeezed into whatever scraps of time and energy are left over.

Wealth changes that equation. Suddenly, your vision isn't competing with your survival—it becomes a priority in its own right. The things you've long wanted to create—a documentary about an overlooked story, a community arts centre, a book series that shifts perspectives, a sustainable product line that challenges waste culture—don't have to be compromised or watered down to fit a tight budget. You can bring them to life exactly as you imagined, without diluting their purpose to appeal to the lowest common denominator.

The reason this matters isn't just creative satisfaction—it's legacy. Personal projects rooted in your values are more than passion work; they are statements of who you are and what you believe in. They outlive you. They speak for you when you're not in the room. They remind others that it's possible to build something in alignment with your principles, even when the world rewards shortcuts and conformity.

When you have the means, you can refuse the false trade-offs between impact and viability. You can hire the best people to collaborate—not just the most affordable. You can choose quality materials, sustainable practices, and ethical partnerships without watching the cost column dictate every decision. You can take the time to refine, to test, to improve, until the finished project truly matches your inner standard.

And there's another layer: your work can exist outside the pressure of immediate profit. Many projects with transformative potential die because they can't "pay for themselves" fast enough. Wealth gives you the patience to let your creation find its audience, grow at the right pace, and stay true to its message. It allows you to take creative risks that may not fit market formulas but resonate deeply with the people they're meant to reach.

The importance here is not vanity—it's authenticity. A world full of underfunded, half-realised visions is a world where innovation and beauty are constantly compromised. When you have both the resources and the will, you can protect your vision from being chipped away by the compromises that come with scarcity. You can give it the chance to exist exactly as it was meant to.

In the end, funding personal projects is about reclaiming ownership of your ideas and showing that values and vision are not luxuries—they're necessities for meaningful creation. When you have the wealth to make them real, you turn "someday" into now, and you give the world something it wouldn't have had without you. That is power. That is purpose. And that is why it matters.

50. What could you create that would make you proud to put your name on it?

Your name is more than a label—it's the signature on the story of your life. Every project, every collaboration, every act of creation adds another line to that story. When you have the financial freedom to choose what you work on, you also gain the ability to decide exactly what your name will stand for. And that changes everything.

In a world where much of what we do is driven by obligation, necessity, or compromise, there's a rare dignity in producing something you'd be proud to introduce as "mine." It might be a groundbreaking invention, an inspiring book, a company that redefines ethical business, or an organisation that solves a problem most people had given up on. Whatever form it takes, it carries a weight beyond the object or service itself—it becomes a reflection of your standards, your courage, and your principles.

Wealth gives you the space to pursue this kind of work without bending under the pressure to make quick compromises. You can take the extra months to refine the design instead of rushing to market. You can hire people whose ethics match their talent. You can reject investors who want to dilute the mission in exchange for faster returns. You can build something with integrity, knowing it will outlast the short-term wins most people settle for.

And pride here isn't about ego—it's about alignment. It's about looking at your creation and knowing it's free from the shortcuts, half-measures, and moral concessions that often come with survival-driven decisions. It's knowing that if your work were put on display for the world to examine—your children, your mentors, even strangers—you'd welcome the scrutiny because every part of it reflects your highest intentions.

That kind of pride becomes its own currency. It draws the right collaborators, customers, and communities to you—not because you chased them, but because the integrity of your work resonates. People can feel when something has been made with care, thought, and vision. And those are the things that endure.

There's also a deeper human truth here: what we create shapes us as much as we shape it. When you set out to build something worthy of your name, you inevitably grow into the person capable of making it. You sharpen your discipline, your resilience, and your creativity. You stretch into new roles—leader, innovator, steward of your own values. In this way, the journey of creation becomes as defining as the finished work itself.

In the end, the importance of creating something worthy of your name is that it becomes part of your permanent story. Trends fade. Markets shift. But the things you make with conviction, care, and clarity remain as proof of what mattered to you and how you chose to show up in the world. When you have the wealth to make those choices freely, you stop leaving your legacy to chance—you write it, one creation at a time.

51. How might you prove to yourself that success can be achieved ethically?

In a world where headlines often celebrate profit without questioning the path taken to earn it, proving to yourself that success can be achieved ethically is more than a personal victory—it's a quiet revolution. It's evidence that the stories we're told about business being a game of ruthless winners and crushed losers are not the only truth.

When you succeed without compromising your integrity, you validate the idea that it is possible to thrive without leaving harm in your wake. You show that values like honesty, fairness, transparency, and compassion are not weaknesses to be "managed" but strengths to be leveraged. That knowledge is deeply liberating—not just because it affirms who you are, but because it frees you from the fear that your morality will be the price of your ambitions.

Wealth plays a crucial role here because it removes the desperation that so often pushes people toward corners they would otherwise never cut. When you're not in survival mode, you can make choices from a place of abundance rather than scarcity. You can walk away from deals that look profitable but feel wrong. You can take the longer route to growth if it means your conscience remains intact. And each of those decisions becomes part of the proof you're building for yourself: that you can do this your way.

The significance goes beyond your own satisfaction. When you demonstrate that ethical success is possible, you create a new point of reference for others—especially those coming up behind you. Colleagues, peers, mentees, even competitors will notice that you refused the shortcuts and still achieved results worth celebrating. Your example chips away at the cynicism that has convinced too many people that "everyone" has to compromise to get ahead.

There's also the internal reward. Knowing that your achievements weren't purchased at the cost of your values gives you a kind of peace no financial figure can match. It allows you to look in the mirror—or into the eyes of those who know your journey—and feel proud not just of what you've done, but of how you've done it. You own your success fully because there are no hidden stains on it.

In this way, proving ethical success isn't only about the end result; it's about living each chapter of your story in a way that you'll never have to rewrite. It's about rejecting the false choice between being good and being great. It's about redefining success so that the process is part of the prize.

And perhaps most importantly, it's about claiming the right to be both ambitious and principled without apology. That is the kind of victory that lasts—not just for you, but for everyone who sees that it can be done.

52. How could you redefine what being rich means for you personally?

For most of the world, "rich" has been reduced to a number. A certain income, a certain net worth, a certain house or car or postcode. But numbers are hollow if they're not attached to meaning. Redefining what being rich means for you personally is about reclaiming that word from the shallow metrics of other people's standards—and filling it with the things that make your life feel truly abundant.

Wealth, when defined by the crowd, is fragile. It's always a moving target—there's always someone with more. When you define it for yourself, it becomes unshakeable, because its foundation isn't comparison but alignment. Your version of "rich" might be being able to pick your kids up from school every day. Or living close enough to the ocean to hear the tide from your window. Or having the resources to fund the causes that keep you awake at night until they're addressed.

This redefinition matters because it guards you from chasing someone else's dream while neglecting your own. Without clarity, it's easy to spend decades climbing the ladder, only to realise it was leaning against the wrong wall. But when you've consciously decided what richness means for you, every step you take moves you toward a life you actually want—not one you've been sold.

It also liberates you from the constant race for "more." If your version of wealth is grounded in freedom, health, relationships, and the ability to contribute, then the goal is no longer to endlessly accumulate, but to nurture and protect those elements. Your bank balance becomes a tool, not a scoreboard. And that shift allows you to enjoy your wealth instead of being consumed by the pursuit of it.

There's a deeper ripple effect, too. When you live out a personal definition of rich, you challenge the default narrative around success. You make it visible that someone can be "rich" in laughter, in time, in generosity, in curiosity—and that those forms of wealth are as legitimate as a financial portfolio. You give permission to others to measure their lives in ways that honour their values, rather than the marketplace's values.

Financial resources amplify this redefinition because they allow you to craft your life without being trapped by necessity. But the key is that the resources serve the vision, not the other way around. If being rich means being deeply present for your children, you might choose work that allows for flexibility over constant expansion. If it means constant learning, you might invest in courses, mentors, and travel rather than in status symbols.

Ultimately, redefining what being rich means for you is about sovereignty. It's declaring that you—not tradition, not culture, not marketing—are the authority on what a "successful" life looks like. And once you own that definition, your wealth becomes a powerful ally in creating it.

53. How might you inspire a movement that starts with your story?

Every movement—whether it changes a neighbourhood or changes the world—begins with a single story. Not a statistic. Not a grand strategy. A story. Your story. And when you have the resources to tell it boldly and live it fully, you plant the kind of seed that can grow far beyond your own life.

Your story holds power because it's lived. It carries the texture of your struggles, the scent of your victories, the fingerprints of every choice you've made. People connect with authenticity, not perfection. And when you share your journey—not just the highlight reel, but the stumbles, the doubts, the turning points—you invite others to see themselves in it. You give them a mirror and a map at the same time.

Wealth magnifies this potential. It frees you to tell your story without compromise. You can write the book, produce the documentary, launch the podcast, or create the platform that amplifies your voice. You can travel to the communities that most need to hear it. You can support the storytellers, artists, and advocates who will carry it further than you ever could alone.

The reason this matters isn't just personal fulfilment—it's legacy. A movement that starts with your story doesn't end with you. It becomes something others can carry, adapt, and make their own. When people see that you rose above your circumstances, built something from nothing, or refused to accept the limits handed to you, it becomes a blueprint they can follow. And with every person who steps into their own courage because of you, the movement strengthens.

There's also a quiet responsibility in this. Many people will never have the platform, the visibility, or the financial means to share their story widely. If you do, using it to spark something bigger than yourself transforms wealth from a private comfort into a public catalyst. It says: I will not only rise; I will lift.

And here's the truth: people are waiting for stories like yours. Not just the glamorous parts, but the human ones. They're waiting to see that someone with their kind of beginnings—or their kind of obstacles—can still shape a life of purpose. They're waiting to see that wealth can be a tool for connection, not separation. That success can be an invitation, not a fortress.

When you invest in sharing your story well, you invest in the possibility that someone, somewhere, will hear it at exactly the moment they need it—and choose a braver path because of it. And when enough people make that choice, a movement begins.

Wealth can buy comfort. But when paired with courage, it can buy reach. And when your story has reach, it has the power to change not only the way people see you, but the way they see themselves. That's when your life stops being just a personal journey and becomes a spark in something far greater.

54. What awards or recognition could you achieve with the right resources?

Recognition is not about ego—it's about impact being seen, amplified, and multiplied. When your work is acknowledged publicly, it travels further than you could ever push it on your own. Awards and recognition are signals to the world that what you're doing matters, and with the right resources, you can position yourself to create work that earns that kind of spotlight.

The deeper reason this matters is that recognition opens doors—not just for you, but for your ideas, your cause, and the people you represent. When you stand on a stage accepting an award, you aren't just holding a trophy. You're holding a microphone that carries your message to rooms you might never have entered otherwise. And the more visible your recognition, the more weight your voice carries in influencing change.

Resources transform this potential in profound ways. They give you the ability to pursue excellence without compromise—to fund the research that proves your idea, to hire the team that turns vision into reality, to access the platforms where gatekeepers gather. Recognition rarely comes from doing more of what everyone else is doing; it comes from pushing boundaries. Wealth buys you the freedom to take those creative risks without fear of survival hanging over you.

There's also a symbolic power in recognition. For people watching from the sidelines—especially those from underrepresented backgrounds—seeing someone like you win isn't just inspiring; it's evidence. It tells them that the system is not impenetrable, that talent and perseverance paired with resources can break through barriers. Your win becomes a shared win.

Awards also have a multiplying effect. Once recognised, your work gains credibility that attracts collaborators, investors, and supporters who might have been sceptical before. That credibility can secure larger platforms, more ambitious projects, and opportunities that would have seemed unreachable in the past.

But perhaps the most meaningful aspect is what happens after the applause fades. Recognition creates a record. It etches your contribution into the collective memory of your industry, your community, or even history itself. And that record—especially when backed by the resources to sustain your work—can keep influencing long after you've moved on to new challenges.

This isn't about chasing accolades for the sake of vanity. It's about using them strategically as amplifiers for your mission. The right award can make decision-makers listen, attract the attention of global media, or convince funders to back your next bold step. With resources, you can aim not only to win but to win in ways that shift culture, redefine standards, and set examples worth following.

When you pair purpose with the ability to execute at the highest level, recognition becomes inevitable. And when recognition arrives, it becomes a lever—one that can lift your ideas, your cause, and countless others higher than they could have risen without you. Wealth doesn't just make that possible; it makes it sustainable.

55. How might you become a thought leader in your field?

Becoming a thought leader isn't about having the loudest voice—it's about having the clearest one. It's about being the person others look to when they want truth stripped of noise, vision unclouded by trends, and guidance grounded in both wisdom and courage. Thought leadership is influence at its purest, and with the right resources, you can wield it in a way that shapes not just conversations, but the course of an entire field.

The reason this matters is that ideas are fragile without amplification. Even the most transformative insights can wither in obscurity if they never reach the right ears. Wealth gives you the reach to ensure your voice isn't confined to a small circle—it gives you access to stages, publications, networks, and audiences that can carry your ideas far beyond your immediate grasp.

But it's not just about scale—it's about depth. With resources, you can afford the time to think deeply, research thoroughly, and speak from a place of authority that isn't rushed or compromised by the need to simply "keep the lights on." You can fund studies that prove your perspective, collaborate with innovators whose expertise strengthens your argument, and produce work polished enough to stand alongside the best in the world.

True thought leadership also demands consistency. It's not a single viral moment—it's a sustained body of work that proves you've not only identified where the world is going but have helped steer it there. Resources enable that consistency. They let you show up again and again with quality content, original thinking, and solutions that are as actionable as they are inspiring.

And there's another layer—responsibility. When you're seen as a thought leader, you set the tone for those coming after you. Your influence shapes norms, values, and expectations. Without resources, it's easy for even the most ethical leaders to burn out, compromise, or be drowned out by those with deeper pockets but weaker principles. Wealth safeguards your ability to stay true to your values while keeping pace with the demands of leadership.

Most importantly, thought leadership backed by resources has the power to spark movements. It's the difference between giving a speech to a small room and broadcasting a vision to the world. It's the ability to not only point to the future but to actively fund the building of it. And when you can do both—speak and act—you become more than a commentator; you become a catalyst.

In the end, the title "thought leader" isn't given—it's earned through relentless clarity, vision, and service to your field. But resources make that journey faster, more sustainable, and more impactful. They give you the platform, the stamina, and the reach to ensure your ideas don't just echo—they endure.

56. How could you create iconic work that becomes your signature contribution?

There is something timeless about the idea of creating a piece of work so unique, so resonant, that it becomes part of your personal signature—something people point to years from now and say, "That's theirs. No one else could have made it." This is not about chasing fleeting applause. It's about shaping a legacy that feels inevitable when people look back on your life's arc.

The reason this matters so deeply is because our creative output—whether it's a book, a business, a piece of art, a revolutionary product, or a social movement—is the most visible proof of our values and vision. Long after conversations fade and titles are forgotten, it's the tangible impact of what you built that remains. Iconic work outlives you, whispering your message to generations you will never meet.

Wealth amplifies your capacity to pursue this kind of work in its purest form. Without the constant pressure to monetize quickly or cut corners for survival, you gain the freedom to refine an idea until it's worthy of your name. You can immerse yourself in research, collaborate with the most skilled minds in the world, and source the best materials—whether literal or metaphorical—to bring your vision to life. Excellence is rarely rushed; resources buy you the luxury of patience.

And then there's the courage factor. Creating iconic work often means breaking from convention, resisting the gravitational pull of "how it's always been done." This path can be risky—financially, reputationally, even emotionally. But when you're not tethered to the fear of financial ruin, you can take those risks with conviction. You can invest in the bold, untested, or unconventional ideas that might fail spectacularly… or succeed in ways that redefine your entire field.

Wealth also allows you to scale the reach of your signature work so it touches not just a select few but a vast and diverse audience. It's the ability to publish in multiple languages, to launch globally rather than locally, to present in venues and markets that would otherwise be out of reach. Iconic work is not only what you create—it's how far it travels.

Most of all, creating a signature contribution is about alignment. It's about ensuring that the work you put into the world is a reflection of your truest self—the values you stand for, the causes you champion, the kind of excellence you believe is worth defending. That authenticity, combined with the resources to manifest it fully, is what transforms a project into a legacy.

In the end, iconic work is a form of immortality. It's your thoughts, your creativity, and your values crystallised into something tangible, enduring, and unmistakably yours. When wealth gives you the freedom to make it without compromise, you gift the world something far rarer than success—you gift it a piece of yourself that will never fade.

57. How might you use your wealth to influence positive change in your industry?

Every industry, no matter how polished on the surface, has its cracks—blind spots, outdated practices, or entrenched norms that no longer serve the people within it or the world around it. To influence positive change in your industry is to decide that you will not merely succeed within the existing rules—you will help rewrite them for the better.

The reason this is worth caring about goes far beyond prestige. Industries shape culture, policy, and opportunity. They determine who gets heard, what gets funded, and which ideas are given room to grow. If you've built wealth in a given field, you hold a position of rare leverage—you can direct resources, attention, and energy toward shifting the entire ecosystem in a more ethical, inclusive, and forward-thinking direction.

Wealth gives you the power to act without asking for permission. You can fund initiatives others dismiss as "too risky," support underrepresented voices who struggle to break in, or launch pilot projects that prove a better way is possible. Because you're not bound by the short-term profit mandates that stifle so much innovation, you can think in terms of decades instead of quarters.

It also enables you to model the standards you wish were universal. You can pay fair wages in a sector notorious for underpaying. You can make sustainability the default rather than the exception. You can treat transparency as a competitive advantage rather than a liability. And when others see that these choices can coexist with profitability, the ripple effect begins.

Influencing change also means creating platforms—literally and figuratively—for ideas that deserve a larger stage. That could be hosting conferences where disruptive voices are welcomed, funding think tanks that explore progressive solutions, or producing media that reframes the narrative of your industry entirely. When you control the microphone, you can amplify not just your own vision but a collective one.

Perhaps most powerfully, wealth allows you to weather the resistance that inevitably comes with challenging the status quo. Industries are guarded by gatekeepers who benefit from keeping things as they are. Without financial independence, standing up to them can be career-ending. With it, you have the resilience—and the staying power—to keep pushing until the change takes root.

At its core, influencing your industry for the better is about stewardship. It's the recognition that your success was not built in a vacuum; you stand on the infrastructure others created. Wealth gives you the means to strengthen that infrastructure so the next generation inherits an environment more just, innovative, and humane than the one you entered.

When you decide to use your resources this way, your legacy expands beyond personal achievement. You're no longer just a leader—you become a catalyst. And while accolades may fade, the shifts you help set in motion can transform the very DNA of your industry, long after your own chapter has closed.

58. How could you invest in branding yourself as a leader?

A leader's influence doesn't just come from the decisions they make—it comes from the story others tell about them. Branding yourself as a leader is not vanity; it's about shaping the narrative of who you are, what you stand for, and why people should follow your example. Without that clarity, even the best ideas can fade into obscurity, overshadowed by louder but less meaningful voices.

When you have wealth, you gain the ability to shape that story deliberately and expansively. It allows you to be intentional in how your values, your expertise, and your vision are communicated—not only within your industry, but far beyond it. This matters because perception influences opportunity. People rally around leaders they understand, trust, and can clearly identify, and your brand becomes the bridge that connects your mission to the audience who needs to hear it.

Investing in your leadership brand is not about personal glorification; it's about credibility and reach. In a crowded marketplace of ideas, your brand is the shorthand that tells people, "This is the person who delivers. This is the voice worth listening to." Without that foundation, even transformative work risks going unnoticed or being misunderstood.

Wealth lets you align every touchpoint—how you speak, where you appear, what you publish, and even the causes you support—so that they consistently reflect your vision. You can collaborate with skilled storytellers, designers, and strategists who ensure that the substance of your work isn't lost in translation. You can place yourself in rooms—both physical and digital—where your message can ripple outward in ways that unpaid or accidental exposure never could.

A well-crafted leadership brand also acts as a multiplier. The more clearly you are positioned, the more your influence compounds. Journalists call you for insight. Policymakers listen to your recommendations. Aspiring changemakers model themselves after your path. This is not ego—it's impact. The stronger your platform, the more people you can inspire, guide, and mobilise toward meaningful goals.

There's also a legacy dimension. Long after your active career winds down, your leadership brand can remain as a body of work—articles, speeches, interviews, books, initiatives—that continues to inspire. It becomes an archive of your principles and your contributions, one that others can draw from and build upon for decades.

Ultimately, investing in branding yourself as a leader is about taking responsibility for the influence you already have, and making sure it's harnessed for the good you want to see in the world. Wealth doesn't just give you the means to do great work; it gives you the means to ensure that work has visibility, context, and staying power. Without that, your potential to effect change risks being lost in the noise.

A strong leadership brand is not about making yourself the hero of the story—it's about making yourself the trusted guide who helps others find their own way forward. And when you have the resources to tell that story with precision and power, you turn your personal success into a catalyst for movements that matter.

59. What unique contributions could make your name remembered?

There's a quiet truth about legacy: most of the world will eventually forget the majority of what we do. Titles fade. Awards gather dust. Companies change hands. But what endures—what is remembered—is the impact of a unique contribution that shifts something in the world, however small or vast.

Wealth magnifies the possibility of making that kind of mark. It's not about adding your name to buildings or funding grand gestures for recognition's sake; it's about creating something so distinct, so valuable, and so aligned with who you are that it becomes inseparable from your identity. It's the idea, the creation, the cause, or the transformation that people recall when they speak your name decades from now.

Your unique contribution could be pioneering a solution to a challenge others accepted as unsolvable. It could be shaping a cultural moment that alters how people see themselves or each other. It could be building something—a school, an art form, a new way of thinking—that becomes part of the fabric of daily life. Wealth gives you the freedom to choose the scale and scope of that impact without being restricted by what is "affordable" in the short term.

The importance of making a unique contribution lies in how it transcends personal ambition. When you commit to something singular, you're telling the world, "This is what I believe in so deeply that I'm willing to invest my resources, my reputation, and my life's energy into bringing it to life." That clarity is magnetic. It inspires others not only to remember you, but to carry your work forward, giving it a life far beyond your own.

There's also an emotional dimension that wealth can unlock here. Financial freedom means you don't have to dilute your vision to appease short-term investors, cut corners to save costs, or abandon projects because they don't turn a quick profit. You can remain fiercely loyal to the purity of your idea, ensuring that what you leave behind is not just significant, but authentically yours.

And here's the deeper truth: being remembered isn't about everyone knowing your name—it's about the right people remembering it for the right reasons. If your work deeply changes even a small group of lives, those ripples can extend into places you'll never see. A teacher who empowers one child to break cycles of poverty. A scientist whose research saves lives long after they're gone. An artist whose work helps someone feel seen for the first time. These are contributions that live on quietly but powerfully.

Wealth doesn't create the vision—that's already within you—but it does give you the means to realise it fully, without compromise. It allows you to protect it, to scale it, and to ensure that when people encounter your work, they encounter it in its most impactful form.

In the end, your unique contribution is your real monument—not made of stone, but of influence, meaning, and transformation. And when it's crafted with intention, it ensures that your name is not just remembered, but remembered with gratitude.

60. How might you position yourself among the most respected in your field?

Respect in any field isn't bought—it's earned through a blend of mastery, integrity, and the courage to stand for something when it matters. Yet wealth has the power to remove the limitations that keep even the most talented voices in the background. When financial constraints are lifted, you can play a long game—building influence not through desperate compromises, but through consistent excellence and principled choices.

Being "most respected" is not about being the loudest or the most visible; it's about becoming the name people trust when the stakes are high. It's about being the person whose work is synonymous with quality, whose judgment is sought when others are unsure, and whose presence raises the standard for everyone else. Money helps you achieve this not because it shortcuts the effort, but because it allows you to invest fully in the calibre of your contributions. You can fund the research that deepens your expertise, gather the data that strengthens your arguments, and create the platforms that amplify your message—without waiting for permission or relying on others' agendas.

Wealth also grants you the independence to protect your reputation. You don't have to accept partnerships that clash with your ethics, rush projects before they're ready, or attach your name to work that doesn't reflect your values. Instead, you can choose opportunities that align with both your long-term vision and your moral compass, ensuring that respect for your skills is matched by respect for your character.

Positioning yourself among the most respected in your field also means creating a body of work that is undeniably yours. Financial resources allow you to refine your craft to its highest form, experiment with bold ideas, and take risks that others shy away from—not recklessly, but strategically, knowing you can weather the learning curve without sacrificing your livelihood. Over time, this willingness to innovate while delivering consistent excellence sets you apart as someone who shapes the field rather than simply operating within it.

But perhaps most importantly, respect grows when your success becomes a platform for elevating others. With wealth, you can mentor emerging talent, open doors for people who might otherwise be overlooked, and support initiatives that strengthen the profession as a whole. This generosity—backed by real resources—creates a legacy of influence rooted not just in what you've accomplished, but in how you've helped others rise.

In the end, being positioned among the most respected isn't about chasing a title—it's about earning a place in the collective memory of your field as someone who consistently raised the bar. Money simply allows you to pursue that path without compromise, to match your ambition with execution, and to build a reputation so strong that it outlives the accolades.

Respect, when earned this way, becomes a currency more enduring than wealth itself. It is the quiet assurance that your name, your work, and your values will continue to command trust—long after you've stepped away from the stage.

Conclusion

Significance is not measured by the size of your bank account but by the size of your contribution. Yet money, when used with intention, is a powerful tool to magnify your influence and to ensure your work reaches the people it's meant to serve. It gives you the means to live boldly, create authentically, and lead with integrity.

And as you step into your power as a unique voice in the world, a natural next step emerges—the desire to keep growing. Because true significance is not static; it evolves as you do. Which brings us to the next chapter—Growth—where we explore how financial freedom can unlock your potential to learn, evolve, and expand without limit.

Section 5 — Growth

The personal evolution that comes from expanding your skills, knowledge, and horizons.

Introduction

Growth is the heartbeat of a meaningful life. Without it, even the most comfortable circumstances become stagnant. Human beings are wired for progress—we thrive when we are learning, stretching, and expanding beyond our current limits. Yet growth often demands two things many people lack: time and resources.

When your finances are strained, your mental energy is consumed by survival. Dreams of learning a new skill, exploring a new field, or travelling to broaden your perspective are postponed indefinitely. You may tell yourself you'll "get to it later," but later rarely comes without intention.

Financial freedom changes this entirely. It buys you time—precious, unrepeatable hours you can devote to pursuits that enrich your mind and spirit. It gives you the freedom to seek out the best teachers, the most transformative experiences, and the environments that challenge you to think bigger. With abundance, you can say yes to seminars across the globe, to world-class coaching, to degrees and certifications that elevate your expertise. You can immerse yourself in cultures, languages, and perspectives that would otherwise be out of reach.

But the real gift of growth through wealth is not in the accolades or achievements—it's in who you become in the process. As you expand your knowledge and abilities, you build confidence. As you push past comfort zones, you strengthen resilience. You begin to realise that your potential was never fixed; it grows in proportion to the risks you take and the opportunities you embrace.

This isn't about collecting skills for the sake of it—it's about becoming the fullest version of yourself. Every investment in your growth multiplies your ability to contribute, to lead, and to live a life that feels deeply aligned with your values. Financial abundance simply removes the barriers so that the only limits you face are the ones you choose.

61. How could financial freedom give you more time to focus on self-development?

Time is the rarest currency. You can earn more money, build more networks, even repair more opportunities—but you cannot create more hours. That's why financial freedom is not just about comfort; it's about reclaiming the most finite resource you have so that your own growth is no longer pushed to the edges of your life.

Without the pressure of chasing every paycheque to meet immediate needs, your days open up in ways that most people never experience. Self-development—whether through learning, reflection, or practice—requires sustained focus. It's not something that can be squeezed into the leftover minutes of a life dominated by survival mode. Financial stability replaces that constant, low-level hum of worry with a calm that makes deep work possible.

With money no longer dictating every decision, you gain the power to deliberately shape your schedule around becoming the best version of yourself. You can set aside uninterrupted blocks for study, writing, or creative work without fearing that this choice will cost you your security. You can attend workshops, retreats, or courses in distant places because you're not tethered to a rigid work structure. You can even take sabbaticals—extended seasons of growth that allow you to break from routine, absorb new perspectives, and return to your work and life with greater clarity.

Financial freedom also enables you to engage with higher-calibre learning experiences. You can choose mentors who challenge you to think bigger, travel to immerse yourself in environments that expand your worldview, or access resources that sharpen your expertise. When you are no longer forced to accept "good enough," you can seek out the very best—and that choice accelerates your growth in ways shortcuts never can.

More subtly, wealth gives you the space for the kind of inner development that cannot be rushed. Reading widely without distraction. Journaling not because you're told to, but because you finally have the mental quiet to listen to yourself. Exploring philosophy, psychology, spirituality, or the arts without feeling guilty for "wasting time." This deep nourishment is what allows outer success to be matched by inner substance.

And there's another, often overlooked dimension: the emotional permission to evolve. When your survival is secured, you can experiment with new ideas and identities without the fear that failure will take everything from you. You can try a new career, dive into an unfamiliar skill, or explore passions you've long postponed—not because you're guaranteed success, but because you can afford to grow through the trial and error that success demands.

Ultimately, financial freedom shifts self-development from being an indulgence to being a non-negotiable. It tells you that your growth matters—not someday, but now. Because when you have the time to invest in yourself fully, you don't just create a better life for you; you become a stronger, wiser, more capable person for everyone whose lives you touch.

62. How might your creativity flourish without the constraints of financial stress?

Creativity is like a delicate flame—it burns brightest when it's fed with oxygen, not smothered by the thick smoke of constant financial worry. When you are in survival mode, every thought, no matter how inspired, is weighed against the question: But how will I pay for this? That mental taxation kills more dreams than lack of talent ever could.

Financial stress doesn't just limit your resources—it shrinks your imagination. It forces you to make decisions from a place of scarcity, to default to the safe and the familiar because you can't risk losing what little you have. This creates a feedback loop: the less you risk, the less you create, and the less you create, the more trapped you feel in the conditions that limit you.

When wealth or financial freedom removes that constraint, it's as though the locks on your mind are undone. You are free to think without the weight of necessity bending every idea toward immediate profitability. Suddenly, a poem can be written without wondering if it will sell. A business can be built around innovation, not just desperation. An artwork can be pursued purely because it moves you, not because it will move units.

Without the grind of financial survival, you can give your ideas the space and patience they require. Some of the world's most transformative works—whether in science, art, technology, or social change—took years of quiet refinement before they were ready. Those years require not just persistence, but the security to persist.

Financial freedom also allows you to feed your creative well. You can travel to absorb new colours, cultures, and rhythms. You can collaborate with inspiring people without worrying about whether they can "pay off" immediately. You can invest in the best tools, studios, and environments to bring your ideas to life at their fullest potential. You can explore entirely new mediums—film, sculpture, architecture, music—without the fear of failing expensively.

Perhaps most importantly, when money no longer dictates every choice, you can embrace creative risk without existential fear. The greatest leaps in any field often come from trying something unconventional, even absurd by conventional standards. Without financial chains, you can be bold enough to explore the edge of possibility—the place where real breakthroughs happen.

There's also a deeper emotional shift: when you are no longer creating under the shadow of "I must," you begin creating from the light of "I can." Your work becomes an act of joy, curiosity, and contribution rather than just a transaction for survival. This shift in energy is not just good for you—it's felt by everyone who encounters what you make.

In the end, wealth doesn't guarantee creativity—but it gives it the fertile ground it needs to grow wild and unapologetic. And when your creativity flourishes, it doesn't just enrich your life; it expands the world itself, offering new beauty, ideas, and possibilities to others.

63. How could you invest in education—for yourself—at the highest level?

Education is one of the purest forms of self-empowerment, but when pursued at the highest level, it becomes something far greater—it becomes a force that can alter the trajectory of your entire life. Financial abundance doesn't just make such education possible; it makes it limitless.

When resources are scarce, learning often becomes a patchwork of compromises: free courses instead of the ones that truly challenge you, outdated materials instead of cutting-edge research, short bursts of study stolen between long hours of work. But with wealth, the ceiling is gone. You can seek out the very best—top-tier universities, specialised programs, private mentorships with leaders in your field—not for prestige alone, but for the depth and precision of knowledge they offer.

This isn't just about credentials. It's about placing yourself in rooms where the ideas are bigger, the conversations sharper, and the standards uncompromising. Being immersed in such environments changes you. It expands not just what you know, but how you think. You begin to see possibilities and connections invisible to those operating with limited exposure.

High-level education also gives you access to powerful networks. The peers you meet in these spaces are not simply classmates—they are future collaborators, partners, investors, and allies who are equally committed to excellence. The relationships forged here can open doors that money alone could never unlock.

There's also a profound psychological effect. When you invest heavily—both in money and in time—into your own learning, you send a signal to yourself that your growth is non-negotiable. You begin to see yourself as someone worthy of the best knowledge and the most refined skills. That self-perception changes the way you move through the world, influencing the opportunities you seek and the ones that seek you.

And the impact doesn't stop with you. A deeply educated person becomes a multiplier—someone who takes what they've learned and uses it to mentor, inspire, and uplift others. The wisdom you gain becomes a legacy in itself, a resource that can be passed down through conversations, projects, and institutions you help shape.

With wealth, education also becomes lifelong. You're not bound to a single degree or a single moment of study; you can continue refining and reinventing your skills at any stage of life. You can pivot into entirely new disciplines—art, philosophy, science, engineering—without the fear that starting over will bankrupt you. You can stay at the edge of knowledge in any field that inspires you, ensuring your mind remains as alive and dynamic as your ambitions.

Ultimately, investing in the highest level of education is not about hoarding information—it's about transformation. It's about becoming the kind of person who can see the world more clearly, solve problems more creatively, and act more decisively. And in a world where knowledge is power, this kind of education is one of the most powerful investments you can ever make in yourself.

64. What new skills could you master if you had the time and resources?

Skills are more than tools—they are keys that unlock new dimensions of life. Each one you acquire changes the way you experience the world, reshapes your identity, and widens your sense of what is possible. When time and money are abundant, you're free to approach skill-building not as a necessity for survival, but as an act of self-expression, curiosity, and personal expansion.

The significance of mastering new skills isn't only in the skill itself—it's in the transformation that comes with the process. Learning something deeply requires patience, humility, and persistence. It teaches you to embrace being a beginner again, to step into the unfamiliar and accept the discomfort of growth. Wealth buys you the luxury of staying in that space long enough to truly master what you've set out to learn.

When you have resources, you can go beyond the surface level. You can learn from the best teachers in the world, travel to immerse yourself in the environment where that skill thrives, and dedicate uninterrupted stretches of time to practice. This level of immersion accelerates mastery in ways that casual effort never could. Imagine studying culinary arts not just in a classroom, but in the kitchens of Michelin-starred chefs in Paris or Tokyo. Imagine learning a language by living in its native country for a year, absorbing its rhythm and cultural heartbeat.

The skills you choose to master also become part of your personal narrative. They say something about what you value and how you choose to engage with the world. They can make you more adaptable in your career, more creative in your problem-solving, and more confident in facing challenges. Each new ability strengthens the foundation on which you build your future.

Resources also allow you to pursue skills purely for joy or meaning, without the pressure to monetise them. You might learn to paint, sail, compose music, or grow rare orchids—not because they will pay your bills, but because they enrich your soul. In a culture that often values only what is profitable, having the freedom to learn for beauty, connection, or personal challenge is a rare privilege.

These skills don't just stay within you—they ripple outward. The guitarist at a family gathering, the polyglot who bridges conversations across cultures, the amateur astronomer who inspires children to look up at the night sky—each one creates moments that touch others. Mastering a skill can make you a source of joy, inspiration, and wonder for the people in your life.

Ultimately, having the time and resources to master new skills is about living a life that feels wide open. It's about refusing to let your abilities stagnate, about continually stretching into new versions of yourself. The more skills you master, the more ways you have to engage with life—and the more alive you feel while doing it.

65. How could you accelerate personal growth through world-class coaching and training?

There's a difference between walking a path alone and walking it with someone who has already navigated the terrain. World-class coaching and training offer you that advantage—not as a shortcut that bypasses effort, but as a catalyst that compresses years of trial and error into months of focused progress. The importance of this opportunity lies not just in learning faster, but in learning with precision, depth, and purpose.

The right mentor or training program becomes a mirror and a magnifying glass at the same time. It reflects your blind spots, the habits and beliefs you might never notice alone, while magnifying your strengths so you can wield them with greater impact. When you work with someone who has achieved excellence in their field, you're not simply absorbing information—you're inheriting a mindset, a way of approaching challenges, and a set of standards that permanently raise your own.

Personal growth is rarely linear. Without guidance, it can feel like wandering through a dense forest—progress happens, but slowly and unevenly. A world-class coach hands you a map and teaches you how to read it. They challenge you when you've settled for too little, push you when you've stalled, and steady you when fear tempts you to turn back. That external accountability can be the difference between a dream that fades and one that becomes a defining chapter of your life.

When you have the resources to choose the best, you also gain access to the best networks. Top-tier training environments surround you with peers who are equally committed to growth. In such company, mediocrity feels out of place, and excellence becomes the norm. This isn't just motivating—it's transformative. You begin to see yourself differently, measuring progress not against what's convenient, but against what's truly possible.

Investing in world-class coaching is also a declaration to yourself: I am worth this level of commitment. That statement alone changes the way you show up. It deepens your engagement, sharpens your focus, and strengthens your resilience when challenges arise. The financial investment isn't simply about buying knowledge—it's about forging a deeper emotional and mental contract with your own potential.

And then there's the legacy effect. The growth you experience through elite training doesn't stay contained within your own life. You take what you've learned—clarity, discipline, courage—and model it for others. You pass it on to your children, your team, your community. In this way, the value multiplies, long after the training itself has ended.

Ultimately, the reason to pursue world-class coaching and training is simple: it accelerates not just what you achieve, but who you become in the process. It strips away the unnecessary detours, aligns you with your highest standards, and helps you stand on the shoulders of those who've gone before—so you can see further, move faster, and live truer to the life you were meant to create.

66. How might you expand your horizons through travel, learning, and exploration?

The world is far bigger than the routines we settle into. Without leaving the familiar, it's easy to believe our perspective is complete—that our corner of reality is the whole picture. But stepping into a new place, hearing a language you don't understand, tasting food you've never seen, or standing in a landscape that humbles you into silence—it changes something deep inside you. Expanding your horizons through travel, learning, and exploration isn't just entertainment; it's an awakening.

When you travel with intention, you begin to notice how different people approach the same universal questions: how to love, how to build, how to heal, how to dream. A family in rural Japan tending a centuries-old rice field might teach you more about patience than any self-help book. A street artist in Mexico could show you the power of beauty in places often overlooked. These experiences broaden not only your understanding of the world, but also your understanding of yourself—what you value, what you fear, and what you aspire to become.

Learning in this context becomes more than academic. It's not just about acquiring facts; it's about absorbing the stories and wisdom of others. Sitting in on a lecture in a European university, shadowing a craftsperson in Morocco, or joining a conservation team in the Amazon immerses you in knowledge that's lived, not merely read. This is the kind of education that no classroom can replicate and no textbook can fully contain—it engages your senses, your empathy, and your curiosity all at once.

Exploration—whether physical, intellectual, or emotional—also disrupts the autopilot mode of life. You start asking better questions: Why do I believe what I believe? Could I live differently? What would I create if I knew more about how others live? Each answer you uncover shifts the trajectory of your choices.

You realise that the limits you once accepted might not be fixed—they might only be the edges of the map you've drawn so far.

Wealth matters here because it transforms possibility into reality. Without financial constraints, you can say yes to experiences that would otherwise remain distant dreams. You can take a year to live in three different countries, learning their languages and histories. You can attend workshops with master teachers, not just watch their videos online. You can fund extended stays in places where slow observation reveals truths that quick visits miss.

The deeper reason to expand your horizons is that it dismantles the illusion of separateness. When you've eaten at someone's table, when you've listened to the rhythm of their life, it becomes harder to dismiss their struggles or ignore their joys. That kind of connection breeds empathy—and empathy changes the way you move through the world.

In the end, travel, learning, and exploration enrich not only your mind but your humanity. They stretch you in ways comfort never could. They invite you to live as a participant in the vast story of the world, not just an observer of your own chapter. And that expansion—of vision, of compassion, of possibility—is one of the greatest returns on any investment you could ever make.

67. How could you pursue long-term personal goals without compromise?

Some dreams don't fit neatly into the space of a weekend, a holiday, or the margins of an already full calendar. They are slow-burning ambitions—the kind that demand years of commitment, seasons of trial and error, and a steady faith that the effort will be worth it. These are the goals that shape your legacy, yet they're often the first to be sacrificed when life's daily demands leave no room to breathe.

Pursuing long-term personal goals without compromise is not just about ambition—it's about integrity to your own vision. When you strip away financial strain, you also strip away the need to constantly negotiate your dreams against the demands of survival. You no longer have to choose between paying the bills and investing in the marathon project that may not yield results for a decade but will one day stand as your proudest achievement.

Wealth gives you the luxury of patience. You can plant seeds without the pressure for them to bloom by next season. If you're writing a book that demands research across continents, building a company rooted in ethical principles, or mastering a craft that requires years of apprenticeship, you can give it the time it truly deserves. That time—the breathing space between idea and completion—is where excellence is born.

Without compromise, you also protect the purity of your vision. Too often, long-term goals get reshaped, watered down, or prematurely abandoned because the resources run out. You take shortcuts to fit the budget, accept partners whose values clash with yours, or scale down ambitions to something "more realistic." But when you're financially equipped, you can stay true to the original spark that inspired you. You can choose the best materials, hire the right mentors, or take the slower, more authentic route without fear of going under.

This freedom doesn't only safeguard the goal—it shapes you as the person pursuing it. There's a unique kind of confidence that comes from knowing you're playing the long game on your own terms. You're not sprinting to prove yourself or cutting corners to survive another month. You can lean into the process, knowing each deliberate step is part of something enduring.

There's also a deeper ripple effect. When you refuse to compromise on your long-term goals, you become an example to others—especially those who've been told to "be realistic" their whole lives. You show them that it's possible to dream expansively, to hold a vision steady for years, and to see it through without bending it to fit lesser circumstances.

In the end, pursuing long-term personal goals without compromise isn't just about achieving something impressive—it's about living a life where your greatest ambitions aren't eroded by necessity. It's about having the courage and the means to honour your vision exactly as you imagined it, and the patience to let it become everything it was meant to be.

68. How might you continually challenge yourself to achieve more?

Growth is not a finish line you cross once—it's a horizon that keeps expanding as you move toward it. The moment you stop challenging yourself, you begin to stagnate. Comfort can feel safe, but it can also be a quiet thief, stealing your curiosity, your ambition, and the edge that makes you fully alive. Wealth gives you the ability to keep stretching beyond the familiar, to deliberately place yourself in situations that demand more of you, not less.

Continually challenging yourself isn't about proving something to others—it's about proving something to yourself. It's about discovering that the limits you thought were fixed were actually just milestones waiting to be passed. When money removes the constraints of survival, you gain the freedom to take on challenges that excite you for their difficulty, not their immediate reward. You can commit to the mountain that takes years to climb because you no longer have to rush back down to pay the bills.

With resources behind you, you can seek out environments that expand you. You can enter circles where the conversations stretch your thinking, the expectations push your skillset, and the people around you inspire you to raise your standards. You can invest in ventures that demand you to learn new disciplines, adapt to unexpected setbacks, and lead in ways you never imagined.

Wealth also removes the fear of failure as a life-derailing event. Without that fear, challenges stop feeling like risks to your stability and start feeling like opportunities for transformation. You can embrace projects that might fail spectacularly in the short term but will leave you sharper, braver, and more resilient in the long run. Each challenge becomes a laboratory for testing your limits, and each limit broken redefines what's possible for you.

Continually pushing yourself also safeguards you from complacency—the subtle danger of success. Many achieve a certain level of comfort and then unconsciously slow down, content to orbit within the same safe range. But the true thrill of achievement lies in the discomfort of the unknown—the place where you have to rise to meet something bigger than your current self. Wealth allows you to choose that discomfort on your own terms, to design challenges that align with your passions and values rather than being forced into them by circumstance.

The deeper truth is that challenge is a form of self-respect. It's a way of saying to yourself: "I believe there is more in me, and I'm willing to find it." It keeps you from becoming a static version of who you once were. And when others see you continuously striving—not out of necessity, but out of a hunger to grow—it inspires them to do the same.

In the end, continually challenging yourself to achieve more isn't about chasing endless accomplishments—it's about staying fully engaged with life. It's about never letting the spark fade, never settling for the version of yourself that exists today when there's a more expansive version waiting to emerge tomorrow.

69. What languages could you learn to broaden your global influence?

Language is far more than a collection of words—it's a gateway into another world. Each new language you learn is like acquiring a new lens through which to see humanity. It gives you not just the ability to communicate, but the ability to connect, to understand the subtleties of culture, and to participate in conversations that would otherwise remain closed to you.

When you have the financial freedom to dedicate time and resources to language learning, you are giving yourself the gift of access—access to ideas, stories, and opportunities that cannot be translated without losing their essence. You stop being a tourist in someone else's culture and start becoming a participant. You hear the humour, the idioms, the unspoken cultural cues that make relationships deeper and more authentic.

Wealth makes this pursuit not only possible, but richly immersive. You can spend months living where the language is spoken, absorbing it in daily life rather than just in a classroom. You can afford the best tutors, cultural immersion programs, and experiences that accelerate fluency. You can travel without being trapped in the safety of translation, meeting people on their terms instead of asking them to meet you on yours.

The influence that comes with multilingualism is profound. Negotiating a deal, delivering a speech, or advocating for a cause in someone's native language builds trust faster than any resume or credential. It shows respect, effort, and cultural intelligence—qualities that elevate your presence in global spaces. Doors open differently when you speak the language behind them, because you're no longer an outsider looking in; you're part of the conversation from the inside out.

Learning new languages also expands your thinking. Each one carries a unique structure and worldview, shaping how its speakers perceive time, relationships, and even reality. As you adopt these mental frameworks, your own mind becomes more adaptable, more creative, and more capable of seeing multiple perspectives at once. This is not just a skill—it's a superpower in a world where influence depends on bridging differences.

With wealth, you're free from the hurried, transactional approach to language learning. You can take the long view, investing years in mastery because the payoff isn't just practical—it's personal. You gain lifelong friendships, richer travels, and the ability to move through the world with a sense of belonging wherever you go. You're no longer just visiting cultures; you're inhabiting them.

And perhaps most importantly, speaking multiple languages allows you to carry messages across boundaries that often divide us. Whether it's sharing a vision, building coalitions, or advocating for change, you become a connector—someone who can translate not just words, but ideas, values, and hope.

In a world where influence often depends on how widely and deeply you can connect, every new language is another bridge you can build. And when you have the means to learn them well, you're not just adding to your vocabulary—you're expanding your reach, your understanding, and your ability to leave a mark that resonates far beyond your own borders.

70. How might you study under the best minds in your field?

There's a profound difference between learning from information and learning from wisdom. Information is abundant—anyone with an internet connection can find it. But wisdom, distilled through decades of lived experience, tested ideas, and costly mistakes, is rare. The chance to study under the best minds in your field is not just a privilege—it's a transformational advantage that can change the trajectory of your life's work.

When you have the financial capacity to seek out these rare teachers, you bypass the slow, trial-and-error path and gain direct access to mastery. You're not just reading about their insights—you're engaging with them, asking questions in real time, receiving guidance shaped to your unique vision and challenges. The best minds don't just share knowledge; they sharpen you, challenge your assumptions, and push you beyond your own perceived limits.

Wealth makes this possible without compromise. You can attend exclusive conferences, join private workshops, or even arrange one-on-one mentorships that might otherwise be out of reach. You can travel to where these minds are—not just for a brief handshake and photo, but to immerse yourself in their environment, observe how they think, how they solve problems, and how they carry themselves in the world. Proximity to greatness has a way of raising your own standards simply because it changes what you believe is possible.

And it's not only about the technical skills or insider knowledge you gain. The best minds in any field often teach through example—how to make decisions under pressure, how to navigate setbacks with grace, how to sustain vision through decades of change. These are lessons you can't Google; they're absorbed through shared space, conversations over meals, and seeing their values play out in action.

Being able to invest in this kind of learning also signals something important about your own priorities: that you value growth over comfort, and mastery over mediocrity. It's a declaration that you're willing to align your resources with your ambitions, not just in theory but in practice. The financial freedom to do this isn't about luxury—it's about compressing years of growth into months, and transforming your trajectory in ways that self-study alone cannot.

Moreover, studying under great minds allows you to carry their legacy forward. You become a living extension of their influence, adding your voice and vision to the conversation they've shaped. And one day, you may find yourself in their position, mentoring the next generation—not as an imitator, but as someone who has integrated their teachings into your own unique contribution.

In a world where most people settle for learning from a distance, wealth gives you the power to learn in proximity. And proximity is catalytic—it ignites not just your skills, but your sense of what's possible. The best minds don't just teach you what they know; they awaken the best in you. And when that awakening happens, the ripple effects reach far beyond your own success—they touch everyone you will ever influence.

71. How could you use wealth to pivot careers without fear?

There comes a moment in many lives when the work you once dreamed of no longer fits the person you've become. Your interests evolve, your values deepen, or the industry around you changes so much that staying feels like slowly dimming your own light. Yet for most, the fear of financial instability holds them hostage in roles that no longer nourish them. Wealth changes that entirely—it turns the terrifying prospect of starting over into an open door.

When you have the resources to pivot without fear, you're no longer making decisions under the pressure of survival. You can step away from the old path not in desperation, but in deliberate pursuit of something that calls to you. That freedom is priceless—not just because it allows you to explore new fields, but because it lets you do so with the confidence that your basic needs, and those of your family, will still be met.

This kind of safety net doesn't just soften the leap—it transforms the way you approach the new journey. Without the constant hum of financial anxiety, your creativity is sharper, your learning is deeper, and your ability to take strategic risks grows. You can choose internships, apprenticeships, or entry-level roles in a new industry without worrying about immediate pay, because you're playing the long game—building expertise, credibility, and momentum in your chosen direction.

Wealth also allows you to invest in the education or training you need to make the transition successful. You're not relying on free resources pieced together after work hours—you can immerse yourself fully, learn from top-tier programs, and accelerate the time it takes to establish yourself in your new career. And because you're not chasing the fastest-paying job, you can be selective, aligning with opportunities that match your vision and values.

Perhaps most importantly, pivoting with financial security preserves your dignity and self-worth. Many people who are forced to change careers under duress carry the weight of urgency—they take whatever comes first, even if it's far below their capabilities. But with wealth, you enter your next chapter from a place of strength. You have the power to say no to roles that don't align and yes to those that excite you, even if they take longer to manifest.

The ripple effect of this freedom is immense. You become an example to others that reinvention is possible—that life doesn't have to be a single straight line. You model resilience, courage, and the ability to honour your evolving purpose without sacrificing stability. And in doing so, you show that success isn't about clinging to one identity forever—it's about having the resources and self-belief to write new ones whenever life demands it.

Wealth doesn't just buy the option to change careers—it buys the peace of mind that allows you to do it wholeheartedly. Without fear, you're not running away from something—you're running toward the truest expression of yourself. And that is a kind of success no job title could ever fully measure.

72. What innovative projects could stretch your abilities?

Wealth has a way of widening the horizon—not just in what you can achieve, but in what you dare to attempt. Innovative projects are rarely born from comfort zones; they demand imagination, courage, and a willingness to wade into the unknown. Yet the truth is, most people never reach for them because they can't afford the risk. Without resources, innovation feels like gambling. With wealth, it becomes a laboratory for your greatest ideas.

The real power of funding your own innovative projects isn't just about the outcome—it's about the transformation you undergo in the process. These ventures stretch you, forcing you to problem-solve in real time, collaborate with experts you might never have met otherwise, and confront the limits of what you thought you could do. They reveal your hidden strengths and expose the skills you didn't know you lacked, propelling you into accelerated growth.

Wealth allows you to step into fields where your curiosity burns brightest, without waiting for someone else's approval or financing. You can explore technology start-ups, sustainable architecture, social enterprises, or breakthrough art installations—projects that might take years to come to life, but which leave a lasting mark on the world. These are not the "safe bets" most people cling to; they are bold ventures that inspire both you and the people who witness them.

There is also a profound psychological freedom in knowing you can innovate without the crushing need for immediate profit. When you are not forced to chase the fastest return, you can prioritise originality, integrity, and long-term impact. That means building solutions to real problems, not just creating what's most marketable in the moment. It means making choices that align with your vision, even if they challenge the status quo.

The significance of taking on such projects runs deeper than personal satisfaction—it's about the contribution you make to the collective imagination. Every time you push your abilities through innovation, you expand what others believe is possible. You create ripples in industries, communities, and even in culture itself. Whether your project succeeds wildly or evolves into something unexpected, it becomes part of the ecosystem of progress, inspiring others to pursue their own daring ideas.

And when you have the resources to sustain the journey, you can weather the inevitable challenges without abandoning your vision at the first obstacle. You have the ability to refine, adapt, and persist until your project becomes what you envisioned—or perhaps something even better. That resilience, backed by financial security, turns innovation from a fragile hope into a force that can reshape your life and the lives of others.

Wealth, then, is not merely a ticket to comfort—it's a passport to the frontier of your own potential. Innovative projects are the arenas where your mind, heart, and courage meet. And when you have the means to fund them, you give yourself permission to step fully into that arena, ready to be changed by the work as much as the work changes the world.

73. How might you build a personal think tank for new ideas?

There is something profoundly empowering about having the mental and creative firepower of a personal think tank—an ecosystem designed solely to explore ideas, challenge assumptions, and shape visions into reality. Wealth turns this from a distant dream into a living, breathing network that feeds your intellectual curiosity and pushes your boundaries every single day.

A personal think tank isn't just about surrounding yourself with smart people—it's about curating minds that challenge you, inspire you, and expand what you believe is possible. Imagine having regular access to diverse thinkers: a climate scientist who reframes the future of energy, an economist who sees hidden patterns in global markets, an artist who reveals beauty in unexpected places, a historian who connects today's challenges to lessons centuries old. With financial resources, you can bring those perspectives into your life not as occasional encounters, but as a sustained, evolving conversation.

The reason this matters so deeply is that no single person—no matter how brilliant—can see the full map of possibility alone. We live inside our own filters, shaped by experiences and biases we can't always detect. A personal think tank works like a mirror and a window at once: reflecting back your blind spots while opening views into landscapes you never knew existed. This constant infusion of fresh insight keeps your ideas from stagnating and your ambitions from shrinking to fit your current reality.

Financial abundance allows you to create an environment where thinking is not rushed, where ideas are tested without the looming shadow of immediate profit, and where exploration is valued as much as execution. That freedom is rare in a world driven by deadlines and quarterly results. It lets your team pursue unconventional solutions, engage in deep research, and cross-pollinate between fields in ways that spark true innovation.

But the value goes beyond your personal growth—it extends to your capacity to influence the world. A well-resourced think tank can identify overlooked opportunities for impact, anticipate shifts in society before they happen, and develop strategies that position you as a leader in shaping the future. It's not just about having great ideas; it's about cultivating the conditions where groundbreaking ideas emerge consistently and can be acted upon effectively.

Perhaps most importantly, building such a network is an act of commitment—to yourself, to your vision, and to the belief that thought and dialogue can change the trajectory of your life and the lives of others. It's a recognition that the best way to ensure your actions are meaningful is to anchor them in the wisdom of many, rather than the limits of one.

With wealth, your personal think tank becomes a perpetual engine of inspiration, a crucible where creativity meets strategy, and where today's sparks become tomorrow's revolutions. It is an investment not just in ideas, but in the kind of future you want to help create—a future you are fully prepared to lead.

74. How could you develop mastery in a field that excites you?

There is a certain magic in mastery—the deep, unshakable confidence that comes from knowing you've pushed beyond surface skill into a place where you can create, solve, and innovate almost instinctively. True mastery is not about ticking boxes or chasing credentials; it's about becoming so fluent in your craft that it becomes an extension of who you are. And wealth gives you the rare gift of building that depth without the compromises that so often dilute the journey.

When you have financial abundance, you can fully immerse yourself in the learning process without the constant pull of survival tasks. You can dedicate long stretches of time to study, practice, and refine—not because a deadline looms, but because the process itself calls you forward. Without financial distraction, your mind has the space to wrestle with complex problems, experiment boldly, and recover from inevitable setbacks without being derailed.

Mastery is also about exposure. To rise to the top of any field, you need access to the best tools, the finest mentors, and the richest environments for learning. Wealth allows you to train with experts who have already walked the path you're on, to travel to the epicentres of your craft, and to learn in immersive settings that sharpen your instincts and broaden your perspective. It puts you in rooms where excellence is the norm and mediocrity has no foothold.

Just as importantly, mastery demands repetition over years—something that many abandon because they cannot afford to sustain the investment. With resources, you can weather the slow seasons of progress, when results seem invisible but growth is compounding beneath the surface. You can revisit foundational lessons without rushing to monetise, giving yourself the freedom to focus on depth instead of speed.

But perhaps the most profound reason financial freedom matters in the pursuit of mastery is that it lets you follow passion over practicality. Too often, people choose fields based on stability rather than love, and while they may achieve competence, they rarely touch the joy of mastery. Abundance allows you to choose a path because it excites you—because it lights you up—rather than because it simply pays the bills. And when excitement fuels commitment, the journey to mastery becomes not a burden, but a privilege.

Reaching that level in a field doesn't just change your skill set; it changes your identity. You carry yourself differently, contribute more meaningfully, and open doors for others who are still climbing. Your work becomes a legacy, not just a livelihood. It is the difference between dabbling in something interesting and owning a craft so completely that it becomes part of your fingerprint on the world.

In the end, wealth isn't the source of mastery—it is the amplifier. It creates the conditions in which your discipline, curiosity, and creativity can flourish without compromise. And when you finally stand at the summit of your chosen field, you'll know you arrived there not because you had to, but because you chose to—and because you had the means to do it right.

75. What habits could you cultivate with more time and resources?

Habits shape lives in ways most people underestimate. They are the invisible architecture beneath every success, failure, joy, and struggle. With more time and resources, you could design habits that not only support your ambitions, but also nourish your health, relationships, and sense of purpose in ways that are otherwise difficult when you're stretched thin.

The truth is, many of the most transformative habits require consistency and patience—two things that are often the first casualties of financial stress. When survival is your primary focus, long-term thinking is crowded out by urgent demands. But wealth creates space. It allows you to build habits not as emergency responses, but as intentional, carefully chosen rituals that align with your highest values.

You might wake up early, not because you're forcing productivity, but because the morning becomes a sacred space for reflection, learning, or creativity. You could integrate daily movement into your life—not rushed workouts squeezed between obligations, but exercise that you genuinely enjoy, whether that's yoga in a sunlit studio, swimming in open water, or hiking through nature. With abundance, these habits stop being "extras" and become the backbone of your well-being.

Resources also make it possible to form habits that require upfront investment—joining communities that push you forward, subscribing to knowledge platforms, or hiring coaches and mentors who hold you accountable at a higher level. These external structures are not just luxuries; they are accelerators that help good habits stick and bad ones lose their grip.

Time, perhaps more than anything, is the gift that transforms intention into habit. Imagine having the freedom to cook nourishing meals daily, not because you have to, but because you enjoy it. To read widely, deepening your perspective across disciplines. To journal consistently, capturing insights and clarifying your next steps. These are the kinds of habits that create compound returns—not only in money, but in peace of mind, self-knowledge, and sustained energy.

Wealth also allows you to build protective habits around your mental and emotional health. You could weave regular therapy, meditation, or mindfulness practices into your life without worrying about the cost. You could schedule regular breaks, sabbaticals, and digital detoxes to prevent burnout before it begins. In a world where exhaustion is treated as a badge of honour, having the resources to cultivate rest as a habit is an act of quiet power.

But perhaps the most compelling reason to invest in habits with more time and resources is the ripple effect. Your consistent choices set an example for the people around you—children, friends, colleagues. You're not just building a lifestyle; you're modelling what it looks like to live with intention, discipline, and joy. In doing so, you become a living proof that success is not just about what you achieve, but about who you become in the process.

When you have the freedom to choose your habits rather than have them dictated by circumstance, you are no longer reacting to life—you are shaping it. And that is the quiet, consistent power of abundance: the ability to turn the smallest daily choices into the strongest foundation for the life you want.

Conclusion

Growth is the bridge between who you are now and who you're capable of becoming. Without the freedom to pursue it, life risks becoming a repetition of yesterday. With the resources to invest in yourself, you open doors to experiences that shape you into someone with more to give, more to share, and more to create.

And here's the beautiful truth: personal growth naturally spills over into the lives of others. As you expand, you inspire. As you learn, you teach. As you achieve, you create possibilities for those who follow. That's why the next chapter—Contribution—is so powerful. Because the fullest expression of growth is when it moves beyond you, transforming not just your life but the world around you.

Section 6 — Contribution

The ability to give back, solve problems, and change lives in ways only you can.

Introduction

There is a moment in every person's life when they realise that true wealth is not measured by what they keep, but by what they give. It's the quiet understanding that while money can buy comfort, security, and experiences, its most profound power is in its ability to change the lives of others. Contribution is the bridge between personal success and collective progress. It is where your victories become someone else's starting point, where your abundance becomes the seed for someone else's harvest.

Giving back is not charity—it's legacy in motion. It is the way we honour the fact that none of us rises alone. Every step we've taken has been made possible by those who came before us, those who taught us, supported us, believed in us, or simply inspired us. To give back is to recognise this truth and to become that force for someone else.

This section will invite you to imagine a life where your resources are not just sustaining you, but actively transforming the world around you. Here, we're not talking about random acts of giving—we're talking about strategic, intentional contribution that shifts realities, opens opportunities, and creates ripples that outlive you. Because when you give in this way, you're not just helping people survive—you're helping them thrive.

76. In what ways could wealth help you contribute to solving the world's most pressing problems?

The world's biggest problems—climate change, poverty, inequality, disease, lack of education—are not small because the human suffering behind them is not small. They are urgent, complex, and interconnected, often feeling too vast for any one person to influence. But wealth changes the scale at which you can act. It transforms your contribution from a drop in the ocean to a ripple that can become a wave.

When you have significant resources, you can direct them with intention toward areas where impact is both needed and possible. You are no longer limited to charity as a passing gesture; you can fund systemic solutions. You could underwrite research that redefines what's possible in renewable energy or disease prevention. You could back grassroots organisations whose work is too bold or unconventional to attract traditional funding. You could give innovators the runway to develop ideas that might otherwise die in the shadow of financial scarcity.

Wealth also allows you to think in terms of longevity. Instead of one-off interventions, you can build projects that sustain themselves for decades—trust funds for environmental conservation, scholarships that renew every year, community centres that outlive their founders. When the work continues without your constant presence, your contribution shifts from an act to a legacy.

Another reason this matters is agility. Crises often demand immediate response—whether it's funding emergency medical supplies in a war zone or rebuilding homes after a natural disaster.

Governments and large institutions move slowly; wealth gives you the ability to bypass bureaucracy and deliver resources directly where they are needed, when they are needed most.

Equally important is influence. Significant financial capacity often brings a seat at the table where policies are shaped and decisions are made. Used ethically, that seat allows you to advocate for systemic changes that outlast even the largest donations—changes in laws, industry standards, and social priorities. Wealth enables you not just to patch the symptoms of the world's problems, but to work on their root causes.

Perhaps most profoundly, your contribution can inspire others. When people see an individual or family dedicating their resources to ambitious, world-changing goals, it shifts the cultural narrative about wealth. It moves money from a symbol of private excess to a tool for collective good. Your actions can awaken others to the truth that abundance carries responsibility, and that responsibility can be deeply fulfilling.

The importance of this is not abstract—it's human. Behind every statistic is a child who goes to bed hungry, a parent displaced by flooding, a community denied opportunity. Wealth can't solve every problem, but it can tip the balance for those who stand at the edge of despair. It can turn what might have been a lost future into a life fully lived.

Ultimately, the reason to use wealth in service of solving the world's most pressing problems is simple: because you can. And if you can, you have the rare chance to stand in the gap between what is and what could be—and to know, at the end of your life, that you didn't just watch history happen, you helped shape it.

77. How could financial abundance enable you to support causes you deeply care about?

When you care deeply about a cause—whether it's protecting endangered species, advancing human rights, funding medical breakthroughs, or preserving cultural heritage—your passion is already a force. But passion without resources can feel like a voice shouting into the wind. Financial abundance gives that voice an amplifier. It allows you to translate belief into action, and action into change.

Supporting a cause you care about isn't just about writing a cheque; it's about having the freedom to engage fully and meaningfully. When money is abundant, you can fund projects that align perfectly with your values, without compromise or dilution. You're not just donating to keep the lights on—you're funding the expansion of a program, the launch of an initiative, or the scaling of a vision that has the power to transform lives.

The importance of this lies in autonomy. With financial abundance, you can choose exactly where your money goes and how it's used. You don't have to wait for someone else to decide your cause is "worthy" of support. You can ensure that funds reach the front lines—directly into the hands of activists, educators, scientists, or communities doing the work you believe in. This direct connection deepens your bond with the cause and magnifies your impact.

It's also about consistency. Many causes suffer from sporadic or unpredictable funding, forcing them to operate in survival mode. Your financial abundance can be the steady heartbeat that allows them to plan ahead, hire skilled teams, and pursue long-term strategies instead of short-term fixes. This stability is a form of respect—it tells the people on the ground that you see them, believe in them, and trust them to do their work well.

Your support can also be catalytic. Sometimes, all a project needs is a major initial investment to attract further funding from others. Your contribution can signal credibility, inspiring other donors, institutions, and partners to join in. You become the spark that lights a chain reaction of generosity.

But the reason this matters most is personal. There is a profound fulfillment that comes from knowing your resources are aligned with your heart. When you invest in what you love—whether that's a local youth theatre, a global clean water campaign, or the reforestation of a dying ecosystem—you're not just giving money away. You're weaving your identity into something bigger than yourself.

In the end, financial abundance turns care into capacity. It transforms empathy into infrastructure. It means you don't have to choose between surviving and giving—you can do both, abundantly. And when you support a cause you care about with resources that match your commitment, you're not only changing the cause itself. You're changing yourself, becoming the living proof that wealth can be a force for connection, meaning, and enduring impact.

78. How might you help lift people out of poverty through targeted investments?

Poverty isn't just a lack of money—it's a lack of options, of access, of the ability to make choices about one's own future. It's the quiet theft of potential before it even has a chance to be expressed. When you have financial abundance, you hold the rare power to rewrite that story, not by offering temporary relief, but by creating lasting pathways out of poverty through targeted, intentional investments.

The reason this matters is that poverty's root causes are deeply structural. A small donation can provide a meal for a day, but strategic investments can create the conditions for people to feed themselves for a lifetime. By directing resources into initiatives that focus on sustainable solutions—education, vocational training, microfinance, healthcare access, and small business development—you are not merely helping people survive; you're giving them the tools to thrive on their own terms.

Targeted investments have the power to break cycles that can otherwise last generations. For example, funding a scholarship for one young person doesn't just change their life; it shifts the trajectory of their entire family. Equipping a community with the means to start local businesses doesn't just generate income; it fosters pride, independence, and resilience. A single well-planned investment can ripple outward for decades, touching lives you'll never meet.

Financial abundance allows you to focus on scale and precision simultaneously. You can research where your resources will have the most leverage—investing in areas where every dollar creates exponential returns in opportunity. This could mean backing technology that connects rural communities to markets, or funding agricultural innovation that doubles yields while preserving the environment. With resources, you can afford to be patient, funding initiatives that take time to bear fruit but ultimately reshape entire economies.

There is also the dignity factor. When you invest in people rather than simply donating to them, you acknowledge their potential rather than their deficiency. You're saying, "I believe you are capable of building something extraordinary if given the right tools." This is a profoundly human act—restoring not just livelihoods, but self-worth.

Perhaps most importantly, lifting people out of poverty through targeted investments creates a legacy that extends far beyond your own lifetime. The children of the people you help will grow up in households that value education, innovation, and self-sufficiency. Communities will remember the investor who believed in them when few others did. And your wealth will have built more than comfort for yourself—it will have built futures.

Ultimately, using your financial abundance in this way is about transforming hope into infrastructure. It's about choosing to be a builder rather than a bystander. Poverty strips away possibilities; your investments restore them. And in doing so, you don't just change the numbers on a balance sheet—you change the human story itself.

79. What global humanitarian projects could you spearhead?

With wealth comes not just comfort, but a profound ability to step into the role of a catalyst—someone who doesn't wait for change to arrive, but initiates it. Spearheading a global humanitarian project is not about vanity or recognition; it's about understanding that the scope of your resources allows you to address problems at their root, on a scale few ever have the chance to attempt.

The importance of this lies in the unique intersection of vision and means. Many people dream of ending hunger, building schools, or providing medical care to underserved communities. They have the passion, they see the need—but without funding, their ambitions remain constrained to the realm of "someday." Your wealth makes "someday" possible today.

A global humanitarian project allows you to act where systemic failures have left gaps. Governments may be slow to respond, bureaucracies may be tangled, and traditional charities may have limited reach. You, however, can mobilize resources quickly, assemble experts, and implement solutions that bypass red tape. That agility can save lives—literally.

These projects also have the power to unite people across borders. Whether it's creating renewable energy access for remote villages, launching a global literacy program, building infrastructure for clean water, or setting up mobile medical units in refugee camps, the work you fund becomes a shared human achievement. People from different countries, cultures, and faiths rally around a common goal: human dignity.

The beauty of leading such projects is that they don't just serve those in need—they also reshape the way the world sees what's possible. They challenge the cynical idea that problems are "too big to solve" by providing tangible, measurable proof that impact at scale is achievable. Your initiative can inspire other philanthropists, corporations, and even policymakers to step up.

On a personal level, the emotional return on this kind of work is unmatched. There's a unique fulfillment that comes from knowing your life's success has been used to lift others in a meaningful way. It transforms wealth from a private asset into a public force for good. And while money can buy many things, it cannot purchase the deep sense of purpose that comes from changing the course of someone else's life—or millions of lives.

Most profoundly, spearheading a global humanitarian project allows you to leave a legacy that is bigger than your name, your business, or your lifetime. The wells you fund will still provide clean water long after you are gone. The schools you build will continue to teach generations yet unborn. The medical programs you start will save lives you will never meet. Your wealth will become a bridge—not just between privilege and need, but between the present moment and a more hopeful future.

In the end, the question is not whether you can take on a project of global significance, but whether you can afford not to. Because once you have the means to shape the world for the better, the real measure of your success is no longer what you own—it's what you've set in motion.

80. How might you bring clean water and sanitation to those without access?

Water is life—an unshakable truth that becomes startlingly clear the moment you imagine a single day without it. In many parts of the world, clean, safe water is so abundant that it's invisible. We shower, cook, drink, and wash without a second thought. But for nearly two billion people, clean water is not a given—it's a dream. And the reason it's important to use your wealth to address this is simple: without clean water and sanitation, no other form of development can take root.

The impact of bringing clean water to communities without it is nothing short of transformative. It's not just about quenching thirst—it's about restoring health. Waterborne diseases like cholera and dysentery claim millions of lives every year, most of them children. With safe water and proper sanitation, these entirely preventable tragedies vanish. Imagine what it means for a mother to watch her children grow without the constant fear of illness caused by something as basic as what they drink.

The gift of clean water also unlocks time—time that can be spent building a future instead of surviving the day. In many regions, women and girls walk hours every morning to fetch water from distant, unsafe sources. That time could be spent in school, running a business, or caring for their families. By funding wells, pipelines, filtration systems, and sanitation facilities, you are not just delivering water; you are returning stolen hours and rewriting what's possible for entire communities.

Sanitation is equally vital. Without safe waste disposal, even clean water sources can be contaminated. Building latrines, installing sewage treatment systems, and providing hygiene education creates a sustainable cycle of health. It means fewer medical emergencies, less financial strain on families, and a dramatic increase in life expectancy.

What makes this cause so compelling is its ripple effect. Once a village or community has secure access to water and sanitation, everything changes. School attendance rises. Food production increases because crops can be irrigated reliably. Economic activity expands as people have more time and energy to work. Public health improves to such a degree that governments can redirect scarce resources to other areas. It's the foundation upon which prosperity is built.

Your role in this transformation is not about charity—it's about equity. It's about recognising that where a child is born should not determine whether they survive. Wealth gives you the power to erase that injustice. You can fund projects that aren't bound by the slow pace of bureaucracy, and you can ensure that the systems put in place are built to last, maintained by local communities, and resilient in the face of climate change.

And there is something deeply human about water. It's a universal need, a shared thread in the story of life. When you provide it, you're not just giving a resource—you're giving dignity. You're telling a community, "Your lives matter. Your children matter. Your future matters."

Few investments yield a return as profound as water. It's not measured in percentages, but in lives saved, opportunities created, and hope restored. And in choosing to make that possible, you transform wealth from a personal asset into a source of renewal for the world.

81. What peacebuilding efforts could you support in conflict zones?

In the shadow of conflict, the most valuable currency is not gold, oil, or even food—it's peace. War tears through the fabric of communities, leaving behind not only physical ruins but also deep psychological wounds that can last generations. To invest your wealth in peacebuilding is to invest in the possibility of futures that are not defined by gunfire, displacement, or fear. It's about giving people back the right to live, love, and dream without the constant shadow of violence.

Peace is not just the absence of war; it's the presence of stability, justice, and trust. Supporting peacebuilding efforts means tackling the root causes of conflict—poverty, inequality, exclusion, and competition over resources—before they ignite into violence. Wealth allows you to step into spaces where traditional aid can't or won't go, funding initiatives that bridge divides, rebuild trust between communities, and create the conditions for long-term reconciliation.

Think about the children growing up in conflict zones: many have never known a world without checkpoints, armed patrols, or the sound of explosions. Peacebuilding creates a new reality for them. It funds schools where children from opposing sides can learn together, creating friendships that defy the narratives of hate they've inherited. It supports programs where former combatants are given the tools and training to reintegrate into civilian life, transforming potential threats into contributors to society.

There's also the rebuilding of physical infrastructure—not just roads and hospitals, but the invisible infrastructure of dialogue and cooperation. You can fund community mediation programs, women's peace networks, and interfaith councils that bring people together across divides. These efforts may not make headlines, but they make history. They are the quiet, persistent work of preventing the next war before it starts.

Peacebuilding is also economic. Without jobs, hope fades; without hope, peace falters. By investing in small businesses, vocational training, and fair trade cooperatives in post-conflict areas, you help communities replace the economy of war with the economy of life. And because war often destroys access to education, your resources can rebuild schools and vocational centres so that young people see futures beyond joining militias or fleeing their homeland.

Wealth gives you the ability to be flexible, to respond quickly to opportunities for peace when they appear—because in volatile regions, timing is everything. It allows you to fund rapid response dialogue teams, support trauma healing for survivors, and underwrite peace accords with the resources needed to make them stick.

Perhaps most importantly, peacebuilding is about restoring dignity. When you invest in it, you're sending a message to communities that the world has not forgotten them, that they are not defined by their conflict, and that they deserve a future worth building.

War depletes. Peace multiplies. Every dollar you channel into peacebuilding replaces destruction with possibility. It's not just about ending today's conflict—it's about ensuring that tomorrow's children inherit a different story, one where they are not defined by the battles of the past but by the dreams of a shared future.

82. How could you protect endangered species through funding conservation efforts?

When an endangered species disappears, it's not just an animal that's lost—it's an entire thread in the intricate web of life being cut forever. The extinction of one species can set off a chain reaction, destabilising ecosystems and erasing millennia of evolutionary history. To use your wealth to protect endangered species is to stand as a guardian at the edge of this cliff, holding back the tide of irreversible loss.

Protecting endangered species is not only about saving something beautiful or rare; it's about safeguarding the natural systems that keep humanity alive. Many of the creatures most at risk are keystone species—pillars of their environments. Remove them, and entire ecosystems collapse. Wealth allows you to fund the rangers who risk their lives to protect elephants from poachers, to finance the restoration of coral reefs that shelter thousands of marine species, or to preserve vast tracts of rainforest that are home to creatures found nowhere else on Earth.

But it's not just about the animals themselves. Endangered species are often a living testament to the health of our planet. The presence of a tiger in a forest signals a thriving habitat. The migration of whales reflects the balance of marine ecosystems. When you protect them, you're protecting the clean air, fertile soil, and fresh water that those systems provide. In this way, conservation is not a luxury—it's an insurance policy for human survival.

Wealth can bridge the gap between ambition and action. Governments and NGOs often know what needs to be done but lack the resources to do it. Your funding can support cutting-edge research into breeding programs, habitat corridors, and disease prevention that give species a fighting chance. You can equip anti-poaching units with drones and night-vision gear, or back legal teams that prosecute wildlife traffickers so they can no longer operate with impunity.

Beyond the immediate protection, conservation is also a fight for cultural and spiritual heritage. Many indigenous communities hold deep ancestral connections to the species in their lands and waters. Losing those animals means losing stories, traditions, and a sense of identity that has been passed down for centuries. By supporting local-led conservation, you're not only saving wildlife—you're preserving human cultures intertwined with them.

Importantly, funding conservation sends a powerful message to the world: that the value of life cannot be measured solely in market terms. A rhino's worth is not in the price of its horn, but in the living legacy it represents for future generations. A forest alive with birdsong and animal tracks is worth more than the timber it contains.

The urgency is real—species are disappearing at a rate not seen in millions of years. Without decisive action now, many will be gone before the next generation even learns their names. Wealth gives you the means to ensure that "endangered" does not become "extinct." It gives you the power to be remembered not for what you took from the world, but for what you refused to let vanish.

By protecting endangered species, you're not simply saving animals—you're safeguarding the balance of the Earth itself, ensuring that the wild heartbeat of the planet continues to echo for centuries to come.

83. What historical sites could you restore and protect with your resources?

Every stone in an ancient ruin, every carved archway in a centuries-old building, carries the whisper of lives once lived. Historical sites are not just remnants of the past—they are physical anchors to humanity's collective memory. To restore and protect them is to ensure that our shared story is not erased, that future generations can stand where their ancestors stood and feel the weight of time in their bones.

When a historical site is lost, it's not simply a structure that crumbles—it's the erasure of a chapter in the human narrative. Wars, natural disasters, and neglect have already taken so much. Yet with wealth, you have the rare power to halt that erosion, to turn the tide from decay to preservation. This isn't about freezing history in time—it's about giving it a living presence, a place where people can still gather, learn, and connect with the deeper currents of their identity.

Preserving historical sites is also an act of cultural solidarity. Many communities see these landmarks as sacred spaces—whether it's a temple, an ancestral home, or a battlefield that shaped a nation's destiny. Your resources could fund careful restoration using traditional craftsmanship, ensuring that the work honours the original builders rather than erasing their touch. In doing so, you keep cultural pride alive and create a bridge between the wisdom of the past and the possibilities of the future.

There is also a profound educational value. A history book can teach, but standing in the shadow of the Great Wall, walking through a centuries-old mosque, or tracing your fingers over carvings made thousands of years ago sparks a visceral understanding that no classroom can replicate. Restored sites become open-air classrooms, inspiring the next generation to value not only their heritage but also the interconnectedness of humanity across time and geography.

Restoration is more than aesthetics—it's economic revitalisation. Many heritage sites, once saved, become sustainable engines of tourism, creating livelihoods for local communities. They draw artists, historians, architects, and travellers, all of whom invest in the surrounding area. By protecting history, you're also creating opportunities for the present.

There is a moral urgency here too. Around the world, climate change, urban development, and political conflict threaten to erase treasures that have stood for centuries. Without swift and strategic intervention, many will disappear forever. Wealth enables you to act where governments may be slow or constrained—funding preservation programs, disaster-proofing fragile structures, and even purchasing land around sites to protect them from encroachment.

Perhaps the most powerful reason to protect historical sites is that they remind us we are part of a continuum. We are not the first to dream, to struggle, to build, to hope—and we will not be the last. These places are evidence of humanity's resilience, creativity, and capacity for greatness. When you restore them, you are making a promise: that the story of humanity will not be forgotten, that beauty and meaning are worth preserving even when they require patience, care, and significant investment.

Your resources can give these silent witnesses a voice once more. They can ensure that when a child walks through those ancient gates centuries from now, they will still feel the heartbeat of history beneath their feet—and know that someone cared enough to keep it alive.

84. How might you help create resilient communities in the face of climate change?

Climate change is no longer a distant warning—it's the reality shaping lives today. From rising seas swallowing coastlines to droughts crippling farmland, communities around the world are living on the edge of uncertainty. To help create resilience in the face of such challenges is not just an act of generosity—it's an act of justice. It is the recognition that, while no one can control the storms, we can influence how prepared people are to weather them.

Wealth in this context becomes more than comfort—it becomes the power to strengthen the foundations on which human survival depends. Resilient communities are those that can adapt, recover, and even thrive despite disruption. Your resources could help build those foundations: infrastructure that withstands floods, local energy grids that remain operational in blackouts, and water systems that endure in times of scarcity. This is about replacing fragility with durability, ensuring that a single disaster does not spiral into decades of hardship.

Resilience is also about knowledge and empowerment. Climate change disproportionately impacts those with the least resources, not because they care less, but because they lack the means to prepare. Your wealth could fund community education, equip early-warning systems, and train local leaders in disaster response. When people know how to act and have the tools to do so, they transform from victims of circumstance into active stewards of their future.

Investing in resilience is an investment in dignity. Without it, communities are forced into cycles of reaction and recovery, constantly rebuilding what was lost instead of progressing. With it, they can plan—not just for survival, but for growth. This might mean funding innovative agricultural projects that withstand extreme weather, or supporting micro-enterprises that diversify income so one failed harvest does not mean financial ruin.

There is also a cultural dimension. Disasters threaten not only physical safety but the very identity of a community—its traditions, languages, and ways of life. Resilience efforts can ensure that people are not forced to abandon their heritage in the scramble to adapt. Whether it's helping rebuild a fishing village with climate-proof harbours or supporting indigenous-led land stewardship, your resources can safeguard both livelihoods and legacies.

And in truth, resilience benefits everyone. We live in an interconnected world—economic systems, migration patterns, and even global security are shaped by how well communities adapt to climate stress. Supporting resilience is not charity; it is long-term stability insurance for humanity. When fewer communities are displaced or destroyed, there is less strain on international systems, fewer conflicts over scarce resources, and more opportunities for global cooperation.

The moral imperative is clear: if you have the means to strengthen a community before disaster strikes, you have the chance to rewrite the story from one of loss to one of triumph. Imagine standing years later in a coastal town you helped protect, watching children play in streets that would have been underwater, knowing that your investment didn't just build walls—it built hope.

In the face of climate change, resilience is not a luxury; it is survival. Your wealth could be the difference between a community's collapse and its ability to stand, adapt, and flourish in an uncertain future. And in making that difference, you leave behind not just buildings or systems, but a living legacy of endurance.

85. How could you make technology accessible to those left behind in the digital divide?

In today's world, access to technology is not a luxury—it's a gateway to opportunity. Yet, millions of people still live on the wrong side of the digital divide, cut off from education, jobs, healthcare, and the global conversation that shapes our collective future. To make technology accessible to those left behind is not merely an act of modernization; it is an act of empowerment that can ripple across generations.

Wealth, in this context, is not just about buying devices—it's about dismantling the barriers that keep entire communities locked out of progress. In rural villages where a single internet connection could open up a library of the world's knowledge, your resources could plant seeds of possibility. In underserved urban areas where students must share one outdated computer among dozens, you could create spaces where innovation becomes part of daily life, not a distant dream.

Technology is the great equalizer—when it's available. A child in a remote farming community with a tablet and reliable internet can access the same lessons as a child in a world-class city. A mother with a smartphone can run a business, track market prices, and connect to customers she will never meet in person. A doctor in an isolated clinic can use telemedicine to save a life that would otherwise be lost to distance. Your wealth can transform these "what ifs" into everyday realities.

But bridging the digital divide is about more than hardware and wires—it's about creating ecosystems that make technology usable and sustainable. Without training, devices gather dust. Without electricity, they are lifeless. Without affordable connectivity, they are portals to nowhere. The reason your role matters is because you can fund solutions that address the whole picture: renewable power sources for remote areas, community-based digital literacy programs, and long-term service subsidies that keep the lights—and the Wi-Fi—on.

Accessibility also means inclusivity. Many of those left behind are not just poor; they are marginalised—women in patriarchal societies, people with disabilities, elders unfamiliar with digital tools, and refugees rebuilding from nothing. With your resources, you can ensure that technology isn't designed for only the privileged few but adapted to the needs of all. Voice-to-text software for the blind, local-language interfaces, and community internet hubs run by local women are just a few examples of how wealth can turn inclusion from an aspiration into a reality.

The stakes are enormous. The digital divide doesn't just separate people from convenience—it separates them from power. Without access, voices go unheard, votes uncounted, and stories untold. With access, individuals and communities gain the tools to advocate for themselves, participate in global markets, and shape the future rather than merely adapting to it.

Imagine returning to a community five years after your investment, and seeing students designing apps to solve local problems, farmers using satellite data to predict weather patterns, and young entrepreneurs launching online stores that ship worldwide. Technology didn't replace their culture or identity—it amplified it, connecting them to a broader stage while strengthening their local roots.

Making technology accessible is not just about keeping pace with the present; it is about ensuring no one is left behind in the future. Your wealth can bridge not just a gap in connectivity, but a gap in human potential. And in doing so, you help write a new chapter of equity, where progress is measured not by who gets ahead first, but by how many get to move forward together.

86. What role could you play in advancing human rights globally?

Human rights are not abstract ideals—they are the foundation for dignity, safety, and freedom in every corner of the world. Yet in far too many places, they remain fragile, contested, or denied entirely. To advance human rights globally is to step into one of the most profound responsibilities wealth can offer: the ability to influence the systems that determine whether people live in fear or in freedom.

Your role in this cause is not measured simply in donations but in the leverage your resources provide. Money, in the right hands, can become a voice loud enough to challenge oppressive regimes, a shield that protects those at risk, and a platform that amplifies truths others would prefer remain hidden. It can underwrite investigative journalism that exposes abuses, support legal defence for those imprisoned unjustly, or fund grassroots movements that would otherwise be crushed under the weight of silence.

The importance of this work lies in its urgency. Human rights violations are not just distant tragedies; they destabilise economies, fuel conflict, and erode the moral fabric of our shared humanity. When journalists are silenced, corruption festers. When women are denied education, entire communities lose their future innovators and leaders. When minorities are targeted, trust between peoples fractures—and history shows how quickly such fractures can lead to atrocities. Your wealth gives you the rare capacity to intervene before violations become catastrophes.

Advancing human rights also requires a long view. Beyond crisis response, it means building the conditions where rights can flourish on their own. You can fund leadership programs for marginalised youth so they become tomorrow's lawmakers, not tomorrow's prisoners. You can support global networks of human rights defenders, giving them the technology, training, and security they need to sustain their work. You can help shape policy by funding think tanks, advocacy campaigns, and research that influence the international stage where laws and norms are set.

The beauty of using wealth for human rights is that it multiplies. Protecting a journalist's freedom preserves the stories of thousands. Defending one activist can safeguard an entire community. Funding legal reform in one country can inspire similar change in another. The returns are not measured in profit margins but in lives lived without fear, in children growing up with dreams instead of trauma, and in societies that function because justice is not an exception but a standard.

This role also comes with a personal dimension. Wealth allows you to move beyond passive sympathy into active solidarity. It enables you to stand not just as a bystander but as an ally with tangible influence. You can walk into spaces closed to most, sit at negotiation tables, and bring the concerns of the voiceless into rooms where decisions are made.

And perhaps the most enduring reason to take on this role is the legacy it leaves. Long after the figures in your bank account fade into history, the changes you help secure—a law that protects a vulnerable group, a school where girls can learn without fear, a judicial system that delivers justice impartially—will continue shaping lives. In that sense, wealth becomes more than a personal achievement; it becomes a tool for rewriting the human story so that dignity, equality, and freedom are not privileges, but rights every person can count on.

87. How might you improve disaster preparedness and recovery worldwide?

When disaster strikes—whether through nature's fury or human-made crises—it does not just destroy homes and infrastructure; it tears at the fragile threads of stability, hope, and community. In those moments, the difference between devastation and resilience often comes down to one thing: preparation. Wealth gives you the rare power to shape that preparation long before the world's attention turns to the crisis.

Improving disaster preparedness is not simply about logistics; it's about valuing human life enough to plan for its protection. It means building a safety net that exists before the fall. With resources, you could fund early warning systems in vulnerable regions—systems that transform a looming catastrophe into an orderly evacuation instead of a mass tragedy. You could invest in training programs for local responders, equipping communities with the skills to act decisively before external help arrives.

The importance lies in the ripple effect. A single community equipped to face a cyclone can save not just hundreds of lives, but also its local economy, culture, and cohesion. When families can return to their homes instead of displacement camps, children stay in school, businesses reopen, and the emotional wounds of disaster heal faster. Wealth allows you to replicate these pockets of resilience across the globe, creating a network of communities ready for whatever comes.

Recovery is just as critical. Too often, the world's attention fades once headlines move on, leaving survivors to rebuild in silence and scarcity. Financial abundance lets you sustain support well beyond the emergency phase. You could fund reconstruction efforts that build back stronger—reinforcing homes, schools, and hospitals to withstand future shocks. You could support mental health services so trauma does not become an invisible, long-term casualty. You could ensure that displaced families are not just rehoused but reintegrated into safe, thriving communities.

And there is a deeper reason why this matters: disaster recovery is about dignity. When people are given the means to restore their lives—not just survive—they reclaim a sense of agency in a world that has abruptly taken control away from them. By funding that process, you affirm the humanity of those affected, turning charity into partnership.

Moreover, wealth enables you to address not only the aftermath but the root vulnerabilities. You could support climate adaptation projects to protect low-lying islands from rising seas. You could finance sustainable agriculture that reduces famine risk after drought. You could back policies and innovations that make supply chains more resilient, so food and medicine still flow when borders close or storms rage.

Your role in improving disaster preparedness and recovery is also a moral stand. It says you believe no one should face catastrophe alone or unprepared, that the gap between survival and loss should not be determined by the accident of birthplace or economic status. In that way, your resources become more than financial—they become a shield, a lifeline, and a promise.

And perhaps the most powerful truth is this: disasters will keep coming, but the level of suffering they cause is not inevitable. With the foresight wealth makes possible, you can ensure that when the next storm, fire, or quake arrives, more people stand ready—not as helpless victims, but as resilient survivors. That is not just preparation for a disaster; it is preparation for a better, more secure world.

88. How could you fund climate justice initiatives?

Climate change is often discussed in degrees of warming or tons of carbon, but at its core, it is a justice issue. Those who contribute the least to the problem—the farmers in drought-stricken regions, the coastal villagers facing rising seas, the communities choked by polluted air—are often the ones who suffer the most. Wealth gives you the rare ability to tilt the scales, to ensure that those on the front lines are not left to fight alone.

Funding climate justice initiatives is not just about protecting the planet's future; it's about protecting people's present. It's about recognising that environmental harm doesn't happen in isolation—it collides with poverty, inequality, and systemic neglect. When you direct resources toward climate justice, you are acknowledging that the fight for a stable planet is inseparable from the fight for human dignity.

With the means to act, you could support grassroots movements that empower local voices—voices that are too often drowned out by global negotiations dominated by wealthier nations. You could back legal efforts to hold polluters accountable, ensuring that the cost of environmental destruction is not quietly passed to the most vulnerable. You could finance renewable energy projects in underserved areas, giving communities clean power without the health and environmental costs of fossil fuels.

The importance lies in the power of agency. Too many communities are told what their future will look like without being invited to design it themselves. By funding climate justice, you enable them to lead the solutions—whether it's indigenous land management practices that have preserved ecosystems for generations, or innovative adaptation strategies born out of local knowledge.

Climate justice is also a bridge between generations. The decisions we make—or fail to make—today will define whether tomorrow's children inherit a world of opportunity or a world of limits. Your resources can push that future toward the former, ensuring that children in every corner of the world can drink clean water, breathe clean air, and live free from the fear that their homes will be swept away in a single storm.

And there's another dimension—accountability. Climate change is often framed as a tragedy of the commons, but wealth allows you to help rewrite that narrative as a story of collective responsibility. By funding research, advocacy, and public education, you can shift public will and political will toward action. You can make it harder for decision-makers to ignore the human cost of inaction.

Ultimately, funding climate justice is not charity—it's restitution. It's a recognition that global prosperity has come at a price unevenly paid, and that those with resources have the power, and arguably the obligation, to balance the ledger. It is about ensuring that the transition to a sustainable world is not just green, but also fair.

When you fund climate justice, you are not merely preserving landscapes or lowering emissions. You are preserving livelihoods, protecting cultures, and securing a fairer share of the planet's future for all. You are turning wealth into a lever that moves not just economies, but the moral arc of our shared story toward equity and survival.

89. What large-scale environmental projects could you finance?

Some visions are simply too big to live in the confines of a single household, a single neighbourhood, or even a single city. They require scale—massive, coordinated efforts that stretch across landscapes, countries, and even continents. Large-scale environmental projects are the arenas where individual ambition meets global impact, and wealth is the catalyst that turns "what if" into "what's next."

Why is financing these projects so important? Because the most pressing environmental challenges—deforestation, ocean degradation, collapsing biodiversity—are too vast to solve with small gestures alone. While every act of recycling, every tree planted, every solar panel installed matters, there are moments when only sweeping, ambitious action can reverse the tide. With resources, you can fund those rare interventions that have the power to change the trajectory for entire ecosystems.

Imagine transforming a barren, desertified region into a thriving green belt that alters the climate patterns of a whole area, providing food and livelihoods for millions. Picture restoring entire coral reef systems—not just for beauty, but for the fisheries and coastal protections they provide to communities that depend on them. Think about financing large-scale rewilding efforts, where vast tracts of land are returned to nature, allowing species to recover and biodiversity to flourish.

Large-scale environmental projects are also acts of hope at a time when despair is dangerously easy. They tell the world that it is not too late, that we can still choose abundance over decline. They invite others—governments, companies, citizens—to join in a vision they can see, touch, and believe in. They become proof that humans are not only capable of destroying the planet, but also of healing it.

The value lies not only in the environmental outcomes, but in the ripple effects. Large-scale projects create jobs, advance technology, inspire education, and foster international cooperation. A massive renewable energy installation can power cities while training a new generation of green engineers. A comprehensive river restoration can improve water security for hundreds of towns while restoring habitats for endangered species.

Wealth also allows these projects to move forward without being strangled by the slow grind of bureaucracy or the compromises of underfunding. With sufficient resources, they can be executed with the urgency the planet's crises demand, not the pace of budget cycles. They can be visionary rather than minimal, proactive rather than reactive.

And perhaps most importantly, these projects become part of your legacy. Long after you are gone, forests you restored can still stand, rivers you revived can still flow, and species you saved can still thrive. They become living testaments to the idea that when given the choice, you chose to build rather than exploit, to protect rather than deplete.

To finance large-scale environmental projects is to think like a planetary steward. It's to accept that your influence can reach beyond your immediate surroundings and reshape the conditions of life itself. It's to place a bet not only on the resilience of nature, but on the resilience of humanity—on our ability to match the scale of our challenges with the scale of our compassion and ambition.

90. How might you create charitable trusts that grow in perpetuity?

Some acts of generosity are like a meal—they nourish in the moment, but their impact fades once the plate is empty. Others are more like planting a fruit tree—you give once, and it keeps giving season after season. A charitable trust that grows in perpetuity is the orchard, not the single harvest. It is a structure designed to ensure your compassion doesn't end with your lifetime, but instead becomes an enduring force that carries forward your values long after you're gone.

The importance of creating something that lasts cannot be overstated. The needs of the world are not static—they evolve, shift, and often intensify with time. By establishing a charitable trust that is both well-funded and well-structured, you create a mechanism that can adapt to meet those future needs without being entirely dependent on new injections of capital. In essence, you set in motion a self-sustaining engine for good.

This matters because history is filled with examples of generosity that made a splash in the moment but disappeared with the next wave of economic or political change. A perpetual trust, by contrast, is a statement of long-term responsibility. It says: "My care for this cause is not bound by my lifespan. My commitment is as enduring as the problem I aim to solve—and as resilient as the people I seek to help."

The power of a perpetual trust is that it transforms wealth into a renewable resource. The principal remains intact, invested in ways that allow it to grow over time, while the interest or returns are used year after year to fund projects, grants, or scholarships. This means the trust can help thousands of people decades from now who haven't even been born yet. It can protect species whose survival will depend on decisions made today. It can respond to crises we can't yet imagine, with funds already in place to act quickly.

It's also a deeply human act of humility. When you create a charitable trust designed to live beyond you, you're acknowledging that the challenges of the world will not end with your lifetime—and that your resources can remain part of the solution. You're placing faith in future generations to carry forward the mission, empowered by the stability you've built for them.

Moreover, such trusts become symbolic as much as they are practical. They tell a story about the possibility of long-term thinking in a short-term world. They invite other people of means to consider legacies that aren't defined by buildings named after them, but by lasting change in the lives of strangers. They create an enduring example for your children, your peers, and even institutions, proving that wealth can be structured to serve beyond ego and beyond era.

Ultimately, the importance lies in the fact that the problems worth solving—poverty, education inequality, climate change, disease eradication—are not "one-time" problems. They require steady, unwavering commitment. A charitable trust that grows in perpetuity is a way to make that commitment unbreakable.

Through such a structure, your influence becomes timeless. Your values continue to speak even when you no longer can. And your wealth, instead of vanishing into history, becomes a living, breathing force for good—year after year, generation after generation.

91. How could you establish scholarships for underprivileged youth?

When you give a scholarship, you aren't just funding a person's education—you're rewriting the script of an entire life. For an underprivileged student, the absence of opportunity is rarely about ability. More often, it's about the invisible walls—tuition fees, living costs, application expenses—that keep their potential locked away. Wealth gives you the power to tear those walls down.

The importance of creating scholarships lies in the way education multiplies its effects. Help one student, and you often help a family. Help a family, and you begin to shift a community. Given the right conditions, that change can ripple outward for generations. The doctor who grew up in a rural village treats thousands over a lifetime. The engineer from a struggling household builds infrastructure that changes a nation. The teacher who once studied on your scholarship might go on to inspire hundreds of young minds.

But a scholarship is more than money—it's belief. For someone who has been told in a hundred subtle ways that they don't belong in certain rooms, a scholarship says, "You are worth investing in. Your dreams are not too big." That kind of validation can be as transformative as the education itself.

Establishing a scholarship is also a deliberate act of leveling the playing field. It's an acknowledgment that talent is equally distributed, but opportunity is not. It's a refusal to let brilliance be dictated by postcode, family income, or the accident of birthplace. It says that merit should have a fighting chance, no matter the odds stacked against it.

The long-term importance is profound. Scholarships don't just help individuals escape cycles of poverty—they can disrupt those cycles entirely. They create pathways for leadership that might never have existed otherwise. And when recipients "pay it forward," they amplify your impact in ways you may never see but will always be a part of.

For the donor, it's also a legacy of hope rather than of accumulation. Decades from now, your name might be forgotten by some, but the opportunities you unlocked will be living proof of what you valued. Every innovation, every community uplifted, every life improved by your scholarship becomes part of your ongoing contribution to the world.

And perhaps the most compelling reason to create scholarships is this: they turn what could have been a solitary journey of success into a shared one. Your victories in building wealth become the foundation for someone else's victories in learning, growing, and leading. In that way, your story expands—woven into the life stories of countless others who will carry it forward, each in their own way.

A scholarship is not charity in the fleeting sense; it is an investment in human potential. And there are few investments more certain to yield a return—not just in skill or income, but in dignity, empowerment, and the quiet revolution that happens when someone realises they have a place in the world after all.

92. What local community programs could you sustain long term?

The heartbeat of any society isn't found in its tallest buildings or its biggest corporations—it's found in the local initiatives that quietly hold communities together. These are the after-school programs that keep kids safe and inspired, the food banks that ensure no one goes to bed hungry, the community theatres that nurture creative voices, and the small grassroots organisations that respond to needs before the headlines ever arrive.

Sustaining local community programs is important because they are the first responders to the human spirit. National policies and large-scale charities may shape the framework, but it's the local programs that know names, hear stories, and adapt in real time to what people need. When you have wealth, you have the ability to ensure those programs aren't just surviving—they're thriving, consistent, and future-proof.

The value in long-term support is stability. Many community initiatives live from grant to grant, donation drive to donation drive. This uncertainty means they spend as much time scrambling for funds as they do delivering their mission. When you commit resources over the long haul, you give them the freedom to plan years ahead, to innovate instead of merely react, to hire and retain passionate staff who know they can rely on steady support.

There's also a deeper cultural reason to sustain local programs: they are the keepers of identity and belonging. A youth mentorship centre isn't just a building—it's a place where future leaders learn what's possible. A neighbourhood garden isn't just about vegetables—it's about teaching collaboration, resilience, and care for the environment. These spaces help communities write their own story rather than have it written for them.

From an impact perspective, local programs create change with remarkable efficiency. Because they're embedded in the community, they know how to stretch a dollar further, how to adapt quickly, and how to measure success not in abstract statistics, but in real, visible transformation—a young person graduating, an elderly neighbour finding companionship, a single parent getting access to job training.

Sustaining them long term also sends a powerful message: that the people in that community matter enough to warrant ongoing investment, not just occasional charity. It says their hopes and challenges are not seasonal, and neither is your commitment.

For you, the supporter, it's an opportunity to see your contribution ripple outward in tangible, enduring ways. You can watch a struggling program grow into a local institution. You can witness how continuity in funding allows an idea to mature, evolve, and reach more people than it ever could under the strain of uncertainty.

And perhaps the most important reason of all: when you invest in the lifeblood of a community, you help ensure that future generations inherit not just infrastructure, but a culture of care. Long after the buildings change and the donors' names fade, the habits of mutual support and local pride you've helped sustain will remain, quietly shaping lives in ways that may never be measured—but will always be felt.

93. How might you mentor young leaders to serve their communities?

The most lasting gift you can give isn't money—it's the belief in someone's potential, paired with the guidance to help them realise it. Young leaders are the future architects of every neighbourhood, city, and country, yet too many grow up without role models who can show them what is possible. Wealth, when used with intention, gives you the power to change that—to step into the role of mentor, to create a lineage of leadership that keeps giving long after you're gone.

Mentoring young leaders matters because they carry the weight of tomorrow's challenges. From climate change to economic inequality, the problems they will inherit are complex and global. But leadership isn't just about solving crises—it's about vision, empathy, and the ability to inspire collective action. These skills are not formed by accident; they're nurtured through exposure, encouragement, and example.

Your wealth can create the space for that nurturing. You can fund leadership programs that remove financial barriers for promising young people. You can sponsor their travel to conferences where they meet innovators and change-makers. You can provide scholarships that free them from survival-mode living so they can focus on developing the skills that will serve entire communities. In doing so, you're not just helping an individual—you're shaping the future of many who will be influenced by them.

The real beauty of mentoring is that it multiplies impact. One person you guide today could be the catalyst for dozens, even hundreds, of others tomorrow. They'll take what they've learned—confidence, discipline, ethics—and adapt it to their own circumstances. Your time and wisdom become part of a legacy that transcends any single project or donation.

It's also deeply personal. Mentorship allows you to pass on more than professional advice—you can share values, perspective, and lived experience. You can help young leaders navigate the emotional toll of responsibility, reminding them that their worth is not defined solely by their output but also by their humanity. You can show them that ambition and compassion are not opposites but allies.

In a world that often prizes quick wins, mentoring teaches patience and depth. It reminds young leaders that change worth making doesn't happen overnight, and that serving a community is as much about listening as it is about leading. By modelling this yourself, you give them a living example of sustainable, ethical leadership.

And there's another reason this is so important: communities need leaders who understand their roots. Without mentorship, many gifted individuals leave their hometowns for opportunities elsewhere, and never return. When you mentor with an emphasis on service, you inspire them to see their communities not as places to escape from, but as places worth building into.

Ultimately, mentoring young leaders is an act of faith. Faith that the wisdom you've earned and the resources you've gathered can be seeds for a better future. Faith that by investing in people rather than just projects, you're ensuring that change will endure—not because it was bought, but because it was taught.

94. How could you strengthen volunteer networks in crisis zones?

When disaster strikes—whether it's an earthquake, a flood, a conflict, or a pandemic—the first responders aren't always international agencies or government teams. More often, they are neighbours helping neighbours, volunteers stepping into chaos with little more than courage and the will to act. These are the people who become lifelines in the darkest hours. But even the most determined volunteer is limited by the resources at their disposal.

This is where wealth becomes transformative. Strengthening volunteer networks in crisis zones is not just about funding—it's about amplifying humanity's most instinctive response to suffering: compassion. The reason this matters so deeply is that volunteers are often the bridge between survival and despair. In many crises, they are already on the ground before aid organisations arrive, speaking the language, understanding the terrain, and earning trust in ways outsiders cannot. By investing in them, you're not just reacting to emergencies—you're building a prepared, resilient first line of defence.

Imagine knowing that when disaster hits a remote village or a war-torn neighbourhood, there is already a trained and equipped network of people ready to act—because you chose to make it possible. You're empowering them with tools, training, and systems that multiply their impact. You're turning bravery into effectiveness.

Strengthening these networks also means dignity for those affected. Volunteers from within the community understand the cultural nuances, the sacred spaces, the local priorities. They don't just bring aid—they bring comfort in a way that feels safe and familiar. By supporting them, you ensure that help is not faceless or transactional, but rooted in shared identity.

The ripple effect is enormous. A well-equipped volunteer network can respond faster, save more lives, and reduce the long-term trauma that follows disaster. And beyond the immediate crisis, they become a force for ongoing recovery—helping rebuild homes, restart schools, and restore livelihoods. Your wealth in this context is not a mere donation; it's an investment in the very fabric of human resilience.

But the importance goes deeper than logistics. Supporting volunteer networks sends a powerful message: that the people in crisis are not helpless victims waiting for salvation—they are agents of their own survival and recovery. Your role is to give them the means to rise to that challenge, to lead in their own right.

There is also a quiet heroism in preparing for a disaster before it happens. Too often, funding floods in after tragedy has struck, but by then, precious time has already been lost. Strengthening networks now means communities can act immediately, without waiting for permission, bureaucracy, or delayed shipments of supplies.

In the end, the reason this matters isn't just about efficiency—it's about hope. When people see that their community can respond to its own crises, it restores a sense of control in the face of chaos. And that hope—nurtured by your investment—can be as life-saving as any physical resource.

By using your wealth to strengthen volunteer networks, you are choosing to equip everyday people with extraordinary power. You are making sure that when the world shakes, there is already a steady hand reaching out in the darkness.

95. What cultural preservation projects could you fund?

Every community holds within it a tapestry of stories, art, language, and traditions that have been woven over generations. These are more than just relics of the past—they are the living heartbeat of identity. When a culture fades, it's not only the people of that community who lose something; the whole world becomes poorer. Funding cultural preservation projects is not just an act of generosity—it is an act of safeguarding humanity's memory.

The reason this matters so profoundly is because culture is fragile. It can be eroded by time, by displacement, by economic hardship, or by the rapid pace of globalisation. A song sung for centuries can be forgotten in a single generation. An ancient craft, once practiced daily, can vanish when the last artisan lays down their tools. Languages can fall silent. Monuments can crumble. Without intentional protection, entire chapters of human history can be erased.

Your wealth becomes a shield against that loss. When you choose to fund cultural preservation, you are choosing to honour the stories and skills that have shaped people's sense of belonging for centuries. You are saying to future generations: This mattered. This will still matter long after us.

Imagine restoring a centuries-old temple that has stood at the centre of community life for hundreds of years, or funding a program to document and revitalise an endangered language before it disappears forever. Picture the faces of elders who see their heritage valued and passed on, or the joy of a child learning a traditional dance, knowing it's part of their legacy. These moments are priceless—and they exist because someone cared enough to protect them.

Cultural preservation is also about resilience. In times of conflict, disaster, or displacement, traditions often become the anchor that holds communities together. Preserving them is not just a sentimental act—it is a way of giving people continuity in the midst of upheaval. A song, a recipe, a ritual—they can remind people who they are when the world around them changes.

There is also a ripple effect that reaches far beyond the community itself. Cultural heritage fuels tourism, education, and creative industries. It inspires new art, literature, and innovation. It fosters cross-cultural understanding by allowing others to step into a worldview different from their own. When you protect culture, you're not only preserving the past—you're enriching the future.

The urgency is real. Once a tradition is lost, it rarely comes back in its original form. Funding preservation now means we can capture, protect, and revitalise these treasures before they fade. It's about ensuring that human diversity—our greatest collective asset—remains vibrant.

Using wealth in this way is about more than bricks, manuscripts, or artifacts. It's about protecting the spirit of a people. It's about making sure that in a world rushing forward, we don't forget to look back at the road that brought us here.

By funding cultural preservation, you become a steward of humanity's shared heritage. You're not just saving objects—you're safeguarding identities, stories, and the invisible threads that connect us all.

96. How might you create safe spaces for vulnerable groups?

In a world that often feels uncertain, the existence of safe spaces is not just a comfort—it is a lifeline. For vulnerable groups, safety is the foundation on which hope, growth, and dignity are built. Without it, opportunities shrink, voices go unheard, and potential remains locked away. Wealth gives you the power to change that.

Creating safe spaces is about more than bricks and mortar; it's about building trust, stability, and belonging. For a woman escaping domestic violence, it might mean a shelter where she can sleep without fear. For a refugee family, it could be a community centre where they find warmth, language classes, and friendship in a new country. For young people struggling with discrimination or identity, it could be a physical or digital environment where they can express themselves without judgment or harm.

The reason this is so important is because safety is the soil in which possibility grows. People cannot flourish when they are constantly on guard, waiting for the next blow, insult, or crisis. Fear eats away at energy, creativity, and ambition. By funding safe spaces, you're not just providing walls and doors—you're giving people the peace of mind that allows them to dream again.

Safe spaces can transform the trajectory of entire lives. A child who feels secure at an after-school program is more likely to explore their interests, excel academically, and develop social confidence. A survivor who finds support and understanding can rebuild their life and become an advocate for others. A marginalised community that has a place to meet, organise, and celebrate their identity can turn resilience into collective power.

Wealth magnifies your ability to make this kind of impact. You can create safe spaces that are not only protective, but also empowering—places that equip people with tools, education, and resources to move from survival to stability, and from stability to success. Safety then becomes the starting line, not the finish line.

This is not charity for charity's sake. It's about recognising that every human being deserves the chance to live free from constant threat. It's about confronting the fact that the world is not yet fair—and deciding to tilt the balance towards justice with the resources you have. It's about saying, "You matter. Your safety matters."

The ripple effect is enormous. People who feel safe are more willing to participate in community life, to take educational and economic opportunities, and to contribute their talents. They go on to create safe spaces for others, multiplying your impact across generations.

In the end, creating safe spaces is about dignity. It's about the quiet power of knowing that someone can close their eyes at night without fear. And when you have the means to offer that gift, you are doing more than changing a moment—you are changing the course of someone's life.

97. How could you provide resources to grassroots organisations?

Grassroots organisations are the heartbeat of meaningful change. They are not distant bureaucracies or abstract institutions; they are people on the ground—neighbours, leaders, and visionaries—who understand their communities' struggles because they live them. They know every cracked road, every family in need, every opportunity waiting to be unlocked. And yet, for all their passion and insight, they often lack the resources to turn vision into lasting impact.

This is where your wealth can be transformative. Providing resources to grassroots organisations is not about grand gestures designed for headlines—it's about targeted empowerment. It's about giving the people who already know how to solve the problem the tools they need to get it done. These organisations often operate on razor-thin budgets, stretching every coin to meet urgent needs. Imagine what they could do with a steady, reliable flow of funding, access to better tools, or the freedom to hire and train more dedicated staff.

The reason this is so important is because change at the grassroots level is sustainable. It's not imposed from above; it grows from within the community itself. A youth-led literacy program can spark generational shifts in education. A small agricultural co-op can improve food security for an entire region. A women's collective can break cycles of poverty by giving members the means to build their own businesses. These are the sparks that, with proper fuel, can ignite lasting transformation.

When you provide resources to grassroots movements, you're investing in people who already carry trust and credibility in their communities. That trust is priceless—it means initiatives are embraced, not resisted. It means every dollar, every tool, every training session you fund has a direct line to those who will use it wisely.

And here's the deeper truth: wealth in the hands of grassroots leaders multiplies in ways you can't always measure with spreadsheets. A single funded workshop might inspire a local leader who goes on to influence hundreds. A modest grant might keep the doors open for a safehouse that prevents countless tragedies. A set of donated computers might open the digital world to young minds that will one day innovate solutions for global challenges.

Supporting grassroots organisations is also an act of humility. It acknowledges that you don't have to control the change to contribute to it. It's about trusting others to know their own needs and respecting the dignity of their solutions. That trust fosters stronger partnerships, deeper understanding, and a shared sense of purpose between you and the communities you help.

In a world where the loudest voices often drown out the most important ones, funding grassroots work ensures that the right people—the people closest to the problems—have the microphone. It's a way of saying, "Your voice matters. Your ideas matter. Your community matters."

When you have the resources to strengthen these local lifelines, you're not just helping a cause—you're helping an entire ecosystem thrive. And the beauty of it is, the impact doesn't end with your contribution. It lives on in the changed lives, the empowered leaders, and the communities that now have the means to shape their own futures.

98. What partnerships could you build between nonprofits and businesses?

Partnerships between nonprofits and businesses are not just transactions—they are bridges between two worlds that often move at different speeds but share a common potential for impact. Nonprofits bring passion, purpose, and intimate knowledge of the problems they aim to solve. Businesses bring resources, networks, and operational power. When these forces align, the results can be extraordinary, creating ripples of change far beyond what either could achieve alone.

The reason it's so important to build these partnerships is because the world's most pressing challenges cannot be solved in isolation. Nonprofits may have deep community roots but lack the capital to scale their efforts. Businesses may have the capital but lack the on-the-ground insight to use it effectively. Together, they fill each other's gaps—not as charity and benefactor, but as co-creators of sustainable solutions.

Wealth gives you the unique ability to act as a bridge-builder in this equation. You can connect the innovative power of a socially minded startup with a nonprofit that knows exactly where their product or service could change lives. You can introduce established corporations to grassroots initiatives that align with their values but are invisible to them without your connection. You can underwrite the pilot projects, joint ventures, or training programs that make these collaborations possible.

These partnerships also matter because they break down old myths about profit and purpose being incompatible. When businesses work hand-in-hand with nonprofits, they begin to see that social good is not a distraction from success—it's a driver of it. Consumers and employees alike are drawn to companies that demonstrate real-world commitment to making the world better. Nonprofits, in turn, benefit from the efficiency, strategic planning, and marketing power that businesses can offer.

And the impact goes deeper still. Partnerships create longevity. A single donation can help in the moment, but a structured collaboration—say, a business agreeing to source materials from a women's cooperative supported by a nonprofit—creates ongoing revenue, skills development, and dignity for those involved. It transforms temporary aid into lasting opportunity.

This is why building these partnerships is not a side project—it's a legacy move. It means using your wealth and influence to rewire how change happens, ensuring that innovation, capital, and compassion are not siloed but shared. It means ensuring that the strengths of one sector fuel the mission of another.

Perhaps most importantly, fostering these alliances tells a bigger story: that solving our greatest problems requires all of us. It's about showing that the lines between "for-profit" and "for-purpose" can blur in the best possible way—creating models of collaboration that others can follow.

When you have the means to spark such partnerships, you are not just connecting people—you are connecting missions, values, and futures. And in doing so, you become the invisible thread in a fabric of change that will outlast you, woven from the combined strengths of two worlds finally pulling in the same direction.

99. How might you influence policy to better serve communities?

Influencing policy is not just about shaping laws—it's about shaping the lived reality of millions of people. Policies set the rules of the game: who gets access, who gets left behind, what is prioritised, and what is ignored. They determine whether opportunity flows or stagnates, whether communities thrive or struggle. And wealth, used with purpose, gives you the leverage to be more than a bystander in that process—it allows you to become a voice that cannot be easily dismissed.

The reason influencing policy is so important is because charity alone cannot solve systemic problems. You can feed the hungry today, but if the policies governing wages, housing, or food security remain broken, hunger will persist tomorrow. You can donate to a school, but if the education system is underfunded or designed in ways that leave certain communities behind, the cycle of inequality will continue. Real, lasting change requires shifts in the framework itself—and that framework is written into policy.

Your wealth can open doors into rooms where these frameworks are debated and decided. It can fund research that uncovers injustices others overlook, making it impossible for policymakers to ignore the evidence. It can amplify the voices of those directly affected by broken systems, giving them the platform to speak where they've historically been silenced. It can also support advocacy campaigns that educate the public and mobilise collective action—because political will often follows public pressure.

Importantly, influencing policy is not about imposing your will—it's about aligning resources and expertise with the needs and aspirations of the communities you aim to serve. This means listening deeply before speaking loudly. Wealth gives you the freedom to fund listening tours, stakeholder meetings, and cross-sector dialogues that bring diverse perspectives to the table. It

Legacy also matters because it creates continuity. The progress we see in the world is rarely the work of one lifetime; it is the sum of many. When you intentionally craft a legacy, you are joining that chain of progress. You are saying: I will take the baton from those who came before, and I will pass it forward with greater momentum than I found it.

A legacy that transforms lives is also deeply personal. It doesn't have to be grand in scale to be generational in impact. It could be the mentorship that turns a struggling teenager into a confident leader. It could be the community centre that becomes a safe haven for decades. It could be a piece of art or a body of work that continues to inspire and challenge minds long after its creator has gone.

The reason this matters so profoundly is because it shifts the question of wealth from "What can I buy?" to "What can I build that will last?" Money spent disappears; money invested in legacy multiplies—not in bank balances, but in human potential.

In the end, your legacy is your answer to one of life's most important questions: What difference did my life make? If you use your resources with intention, vision, and courage, that answer could echo for centuries. And the greatest measure of your success will not be found in what you possessed, but in the lives you transformed and the futures you helped create.

Conclusion

Contribution is the soul of wealth. Everything you build, earn, and achieve gains a deeper purpose when you use it to create a better world for others. The beauty of contribution is that it multiplies.

The resources you put into a cause today can still be changing lives decades from now. The mentorship you give can echo in the leadership of tomorrow. The communities you strengthen can become the foundation for the dreams of people you will never meet.

And here's the truth—when you give back with intention, you don't lose. You expand. You step into a life of meaning that cannot be purchased in any store or captured in any number. Your success becomes more than personal; it becomes part of the human story.

As you close this chapter, carry with you the understanding that contribution is not the end of the journey—it's the heart of it.

caught in your chest. Next to each reason, write one action you will take in the next **24 hours**. Not someday. Not when the economy warms or the stars align. Today. Move ten dollars into savings. Send the email that might change your career. Cancel something that steals your time. Set the automatic contribution you've been meaning to set. Ask for the meeting. Put your phone in another room and study the thing that will make you dangerous in the best way. Then tell somebody you trust what you did. Success loves witnesses.

When fear returns—and it will—answer it with numbers and memories. Numbers: your plan, your budget, your targets, your progress. Memories: the crises you outlived, the skills you earned, the doors you opened. Keep evidence of your becoming. It's hard to argue with a ledger of small wins. It's harder still to stop a person who is willing to begin again.

There will be voices that say your desire for wealth is selfish, naïve, or vulgar. Smile and keep building. Let your receipts refute them: the families you employ, the debts you pay, the students you sponsor, the artists you commission, the parents you relieve, the communities you strengthen. Let your life be the answer-key to their questions. You are not responsible for their comfort. You are responsible for your contribution.

Remember: nothing in this book asked you to become someone else. It asked you to become more yourself. To bring to the surface the discipline you already carry, the imagination you've been hiding, and the courage you suspected was there all along. Money will not supply these. It will invite them out, task them hard, and reward them well. When you meet resistance, meet it with patience. When you meet opportunity, meet it with preparation. When you meet success, meet it with humility and open hands.

So here we are at the last line of the last chapter, and the only question that still matters is the one you ask yourself when you wake tomorrow: **What will I do today that my richer, wiser self will thank me for?** Choose one reason. Choose five. Choose all 101 if you like. But choose. Because your future does not begin when the money arrives; it begins the moment you take responsibility for the next decision.

This book is not a map to a treasure buried somewhere else. It is a mirror. You are the asset that compounds. You are the strategy that works. If the world never notices your name, it will still feel the force of your choices. If the world knows your name, let it know you by your generosity first.

Close the cover with peace. Open your day with purpose. The reasons are waiting for you in the ordinary places: in your calendar, your conversations, your accounts, your craft. Give them a home in your habits. Guard them with your boundaries. Feed them with your attention. Aim them at the people and places you love.

And then—quietly, consistently—build the kind of wealth that sets people free.

Made in the USA
Monee, IL
04 November 2026

67380854R00125